OASIS & THE TWISTED WHEEL

A 'MICROCOSM' OF THE STREET LIFE & CLUB
SCENE (IN VERSE) IN 1960'S MANCHESTER BY
DAVID PRESTBURY

DAVID PRESTBURY 2008

ALL POEMS, DRAWINGS,
PAINTINGS, CARTOONS,
FRONT & BACK COVER
DESIGNS & THE TITLE PAGE
ARE BY THE AUTHOR

FAMILY PHOTOGRAPHS ARE
TAKEN BY THE AUTHOR
AND THE AUTHOR'S LATE
FATHER ALFRED PRESTBURY

THE ROYAL WELSH FUSILIERS 1914 PHOTO PG120
& RAVENSBURY F.C. PHOTO PG19 ARE FROM FAMILY ARCHIVES

OLD MAGAZINE PHOTO'S OF 'SCOTT WALKER PG77, B.B. KING PG67
AND BOB DYLAN ARE ENHANCED BY THE AUTHOR

FIRST EDITION 2008
PUBLISHED BY DAVID PRESTBURY
IBSN: 978-0-9559777-0-1

FOR -

MY MUM WINIFRED & LATE FATHER ALFRED
MUM'S LATE HUSBAND STANLEY
& PARTNER KENETH

DAUGHTER: LAURA JOANNE

SONS: DAMIAN SCOTT,
NICHOLAS ALEXANDER (& PARTNER LISA)
& JAIMIE LEE

GRANDAUGHTER: ROBYN ALEX
GRANDSON: CHARLIE ALAN

EX- WIVES: LYNN & CAROL

BROTHERS & THEIR WIVES:
PHILIP & CATHERINE,
GLYN & LESLEY,
DUNCAN
BRYAN & SUSAN

NEPHEWS: PAUL, JONATHAN & RICHARD
NIECES: LOUISE (& HUSBAND JEREMY)
ELIZABETH & SARAH

PLUS ALL THE REST OF MY FANTASTIC FAMILY
AND TRUE FRIENDS

- THIS ONE'S FOR YOU!......

TO QUOTE FROM THE BEATLES SONG **'IN MY LIFE'**

"THERE *ARE PLACES I'LL REMEMBER*
ALL MY LIFE, THOUGH SOME HAVE CHANGED,
SOME FOREVER, NOT FOR BETTER,
SOME HAVE GONE AND SOME REMAIN"
ALL THESE PLACES HAD THEIR MOMENTS
WITH LOVERS AND FRIENDS I CAN STILL RECALL
SOME ARE DEAD AND SOME ARE LIVING,
IN MY LIFE I'VE LOVED THEM ALL."

I WOULD LIKE TO DEDICATE THIS BOOK
TO THE PLACES, LOVERS AND FRIENDS
I LOVED IN MY LIFE AND CAN STILL RECALL

SOMEBODY ONCE SAID –
"*IF YOU REMEMBER THE SIXTIES-YOU WEREN'T THERE?"*

WELL I REMEMBER THE SIXTIES
& I WAS CERTAINLY '*HERE, THERE & EVERYWHERE'*
IT WAS AN '*EVERLASTING LOVE'* AFFAIR

THEY SAY IT WAS THE LAST AGE OF INNOCENCE
INNOCENT – US! – WE WERE AS GUILTY AS SIN!

CONTENTS

7 A DAY IN A LIFE (EARLY SIXTIES)

13 1963 - A TEENAGE REBELLION

18 RAVENSBURY F.C. (1963)

20 SCHOOL CRICKET TEAM/ RUGGER

21 TAKEN FOR A RIDE?/THE CUT

22 DAISY NOOK ANNUAL FAIR

23 FROM A JACK TO A KING

24 STAYING AT GRANDMA'S

25 LEAVING SCHOOL

29 SWEET SIXTEEN (A LOST OPPORTUNITY!)

30 RHYTHM & BLUES

32 THE OASIS

33 GROUPS (THAT APPEARED AT THE OASIS)

35 WAYNE FONTANA?

36 LOCAL DRUNKS

37 CHARACTERS

39 ON THE CORNER

40 SHORT BACK & SIDES

41 FLITTING

43 LAST TANGO IN FAILSWORTH

44 TOP TEN CLUB (BELLE VUE)

45 BEAT CITY/THE THREE COINS

46 TOP TWENTY CLUB (DROYLSDEN)

47 JUNGFRAU/LE PHONAGRAPHE

48 1965

49 T.V. (SIXTIES)

55 THE MUSICALS

56 FASHIONS & STYLES

59 MOVIES (THE SIXTIES)

64 ASHTON PALAIS

65 THE TWISTED WHEEL

67 THE FREE TRADE HALL

68 HEAVEN & HELL

69 TIMES THEY ARE A-CHANGIN'

70 END OF THE WORLD (ACCORDING TO LEONARD COHEN)

71 THE MANCHESTER CAVERN/MAGIC VILLAGE

72 SOUL NIGHT'S IN RAINY CITY
75 PHIL SPECTOR/BURT BACHARACH
76 CABARET
77 FAGINS
78 OTHER CITY CLUBS
79 THE RITZ
81 BLACKPOOL
83 THE LAKES
84 ISLE OF MAN (65)
85 GET YOUR KICKS IN YEAR 66!
87 FOOTY
89 BOXING/WRESTLING
90 ASHTON COLLEGE
91 HIPPY DAZE
92 FLOWER POWER
94 COLLEGE OF COMMERCE
95 MARKET ST. MANCHESTER 1963
96 DIRTY OL' TOWN
99 SATURDAY NIGHT HEAVER
100 TOSSA DE MAR (1967)
102 LLORET DE MAR (1968)
103 THOSE WERE THE DAYS
104 ON THE ROAD AGAIN
108 MY 21ST
110 WHEN WE WERE YOUNG (PART 1)
112 THE DARK SUBURBAN SKIES
114 WHEN WE WERE YOUNG (PART 2)
115 PREMONITION
117 GRANDAD/GRANDAD BREAKS WIND
118 THE DAY GRANDAD CAME TO VISIT
119 GRANDAD (OUR HERO)
120 THE ROYAL WELSH FUSILIERS PHOTO
121 YOU, OLD MAN (WITH GREY WHISKERS & CLOTH CAP)
122 THE FORGOTTEN YEARS
124 BEATLES & STONES ETC.
125 'THE KING' ELVIS PRESLEY
126 DAVID PRESTBURY

A DAY IN A LIFE (EARLY SIXTIES)

THE SWEET SMELL OF PEA SOUP (WITH HAMSHANK)
LIVER & ONIONS/BREAST OF LAMB/ CABBAGE & RIBS
& BARLEY STEW (WITH A DUMPLING)
WOULD BECKON US KIDS AFTER A HARD DAY'S GRUEL AT SCHOOL

SCHOOL SATCHELS TOSSED AND SLUNG INTO THE 'GLORY 'OLE'
AS WE WAITED RAVENOUSLY FOR OUR TEA -
& DAD COMING HOME FROM WORK (WHICH SEEMED A LIFETIME!)

THEN AT LONG LAST WE'D ALL SIT TOGETHER
LIKE 'THE MITES OF THE ROUND TABLE'
ALL THE 'THE MAGNIFICENT SEVEN' OF US, FOR OUR SACRED TEA
WHICH WAS GOBBLED UP RATHER GREEDILY
WITH NOTHIN' LEFTOVER - ONLY AN ESCAPED CARROT OR PEA

AFTERS (ALL HOME-MADE) APPLE PIE/ RHUBARB & CUSTARD/
RICE PUDD (WITH THE SKIN ON)/ WIMBERRY TART/ 'GOOSEGOGS'
(GOOSEBERRIES) WITH CARNATION CREAM
WERE ALL SWIFTLY DEVOURED WITH SUCH ESTEEM
& MUM NEVER HAD TO WASH THE BOWLS
-YOU SHOULD HAVE SEEN THEM GLEAM!

THEN US KIDS WOULD RETIRE
TO 'THE BEST ROOM' (PARLOUR)
TO SEEK OUT THE LATEST COMICS -
THE *LION*TIGER*EAGLE*HOTSPUR* DANDY*BEANO*BEEZER*TOPPER*
PLUS THE 'MUNCHIES' MUM TREATED
US TO ON THURSDAY PAY WEEK

IN THE SUMMER HOLS -
WE ALWAYS PLAYED CRICKET -
WITH WHITE CHALKED WICKETS
ON THE GARDEN WALL
A FRESHLY LINSEEDED BAT
AND A LETHAL CORKY BALL
"HOWZATTT!!" - "NEVER!"
"YER OUT 'COS THERE'S A CHALKMARK!
ON THE BLOODY BALL!" -
"L.B.W!" - "NO WAY!
I WUZ OUT OF MI CREASE
WHEN IT HIT MI KNEE!"WE'D ARGUE &
SQUABBLE UNTIL OUR MUM CALLED US IN -
ESPECIALLY WHEN IT WAS MY TURN TO BAT -
DRAT!

ME & My BRO'S —L TO R   DUNCAN, MYSELF, BRYAN, PHILIP & GLYN

THEN IT WAS OFF TO THE PARK 'TIL IT GOT DARK
ROSY CHEEKS, GRAZED AND GRUBBY KNEES
WALLOPIN' WASPS AND CHASIN' BEES
DIGGING UP 'BLOODSUCKERS' (LARGE WORMS) & CLIMBING TREES
THROWIN' WATER BOMBS & GRASS SODS
- SPLAT! RIGHT IN THE MUSH

PLAYING FOOTY - TRUDGING ABOUT IN MUCK & SLUDGE
COWY'S & INJUNS' - WAR GAMES
SHOOTIN', FIGHTIN' & PLAYIN' DEAD

ROLLIN' & TUMBLING
INTO THAT GRASS SODDEN DITCH

THEN BACK TO OUR STREET GAMES
MAKIN' PITCH BOMBS
WITH A LOLLIPOP STICK
HANDS SMELLIN' STRONGLY OF BLACK STICKY PITCH

UNTIL OUR IRATE DAD BAWLS US IN -
"JUST LOOK AT TH'STATE! - WHERE 'AVE YER BIN?"
GROWLING & WAGGIN' HIS FINGER
AND ESCORTIN' US HOME BY OUR EARS,
INTO THE KITCHEN -
WHERE THE AROMA OF THE NIGHT'S TEA WOULD STILL LINGER

'THE LONE RANGER' BRO. DUNCAN

"A LITTLE BUGGER UP THE BACK IS OUR BRYAN,"
MUM WOULD SAY - "COME HERE!!
YOU LITTLE SODPOT OR YOU'LL GERRA A THICK EAR!
AN' YOU OLDER KIDS - GO & SCRUBB THOSE MUCKY MITTS! -
OR YER DAD'LL HAVE FITS"

WITH THE CLOTHES RACK DRIPPING WATER DOWN YER BACK
AND FLYPAPER DOTTED WITH BLUEBOTTLES -
DANGLING FROM THE KITCHEN CEILIN'
- WASN'T MOST APPEALIN'

KNITTING PATTERNS, WOMAN'S OWN MAGAZINES, OL' COMICS
AND YESTERDAYS YELLOWING NEWSPAPERS HIDDEN DISCRETELY
UNDER THE SETTEE AND ARMCHAIRS
AND WONDERS NEVER CEASE -
WITH THE CAT CURLED UP UPON THE MANTELPIECE

AND MUM TOASTING CRUMPETS (WITH HER THREE PRONGED FORK)
ON THE COAL FIRE'S GLOWING EMBERS

WITH THE POKER IN TH'OTHER HAND
GIVING THE COAL AND COKE A GOOD POKE
WHILE TELLIN' US THE LASTEST IRISH JOKE

AS DAD SAT SOLEIN' AND HEELIN' THE FAMILY SHOES
ON HIS COBBLER'S LAST (SOMETIMES MENDING WATCHES & CLOCKS)
US KIDS WOULD BE WATCHIN' 'RANGE RIDER' ON TH' BOX

GRAN WOULD TAKE A HUGE SLAB OF HUGH FAY'S BEST BUTTER
FROM THE KITCHEN LARDER –
TO SMOTHER THOSE SCORCHIN' HOT CRUMPETS FOR OUR SUPPER

THEN ASK GRANDAD TO FETCH THE COAL BUCKET IN
WHO WOULD CREATE A DRAUGHT THROUGHOUT THE HOUSE - BRRRRRR!
"PUT WOOD IN TH'OLE! AND SHUT THAT BLUE PENCIL DOOR!"
BAWLED DAD, SCARING THE CAT (& UNINVITED DORMOUSE)

"SIT DOWN BRY! YER LIKE A BLUE-ARSE FLY,"
MUM WOULD SHOUT THEN GIVE HIM A GOOD CLOUT
WHEN ALL WAS SETTLED, WE'D SIT THERE SUPPIN' OVALTINE
AND SCOFFIN' THOSE DELICIOUS HOT BUTTERED CRUMPETS

ALL SNUG LIKE PEAS IN A POD - BY THE FIRESIDE
WATCHIN' 'WAGON TRAIN' OR 'RAWHIDE'
WITH MUM DROOLIN' OVER 'ROWDY YATES' & 'FLINT McCULLOUGH'
AND GRAN OVER 'WARD BOND', 'WISHBONE' & 'CHARLIE WOOSTER'

GERRIN' US KIDS READY FOR BED WAS A CHORE AND A HALF
WITH OLDER ONES QUEUING FOR A BATH
AND LITTLE ONES SITTING ON THE KITCHEN WINDOW SILL
STINKING FEET DANGLING IN THE SINK
- POOH! WHAT A PEN AND INK!

PITCH STAINS BEING SCRUBBED WITH CARBOLIC SOAP (OR BUTTER)
AND THOSE ENDLESS TIDE MARKS ON OUR NECKS
SPONGED VIGOROUSLY BY OUR MUM – OUCH! OH! HECK!
TEETH BRUSHED, LIBERTY BODICES, VESTS AND 'JAMA'S ON
HOT WATER BOTTLES TO LIE ON, OFF UP TO BED TO DREAM ON –
'COWYS' & 'INJUNS', 'ANDY PANDY', 'BILL & BEN',
SCAREEE GGGHOSTS AND EVIL BOGEYMEN
AND OH! HOW WE DREADED THAT SLEEPY YAWNIN' MORNIN'
LIKE ZOMBIES QUEUING FOR THE OUTSIDE LOO A CASE OF FIRST UP
- BEST DRESSED - READY FOR SKOO!!......

BRO'S L TO R DUNCAN, BRYAN & GLYN — WELL SCRUBBED!

1963 – A TEENAGE REBELLION

FROM SNOTTY-NOSED LITTLE URCHINS
THAT CHASED AFTER FIRE ENGINES FOR A DECADE
(AND BEING CHASED
BY POLICE 'BLACK MARIAS' FOR ACTING THE DICK-ED)

WE WERE NOW CHASING DAMES
THUS OUTPLAYING THOSE STREET GAMES

LIKE THE GRASS SOD RAIDS
WE SPLATTERED AND SOILED

EACH OTHER WITH ON THE CROFT
WAS GROWING UP – GROWING SOFT?

STREET SCALLIES –L TO R NICHOLAS, BRO'S GLYN & DUNC & DAVID

WE EVEN CALLED AN AMNESTY
WITH OUR LEAD SOLDIER HOSTILITIES
MOST OF THEM HEADLESS AND LEGLESS
SUFFERED BY EXTREME BATTLE FATIQUE
FROM THOSE TABLE TOP AND WINDOW SIL WARS
WAGED BY MY BROTHERS AND ME

RELUCTANTLY HANDING DOWN MY MATCHBOX SERIES CORGY
AND DINKY CARS, ACTION MAN SOLDIERS OR AS DAD WOULD SAY
"LITTLE BOYS DOLLS" - TO MY EVER SO GRATEFUL YOUNGER BRO'S

PROUDLY PROGRESSING INTO SPOTTY TEENS
WEARING A TRENDY LIME GREEN MOHAIR JUMPER
(ADORNED WITH STICKY BOBS)
WITH A PAIR OF ICE-BLUE SKIN TIGHT JEANS

KICKED OFF WITH A PAIR OF 'WINKLEPICKER' SHOES
WALKIN' BOWLEGGED, CHEWING ON A LICORICE ROOT
CLENCHED IN YOUR TEETH LIKE YOU WERE SMOKIN' A CHEROOT

EYES SQUINTING, MOUTH WITH A SNEER
LOOKIN' 'ARD AS NAILS - I WALKED WITHOUT FEAR
TRYING (UNSUCCESSFULLY) TO LOOK MEAN

WITH A 'BRYLCREEMED' QUIFF AND A D.A.
- I WAS THE NORTHWEST'S ANSWER TO JAMES DEAN
SLINGING SLUG GUNS - THE WEBLEY ORIGINAL OR SILVER GATT
POTTING LAMPOSTS JUST FOR THE CRAIC

DECKIN' ON AND OFF TROLLEY BUSES
PRAYING YOU DIDN'T MISS THAT SHINEY, SILVER HAND POLE
- TO SAVE FACE AND BLUSHES

MAKING A TREE DEN WITH MY REPROBATES ON CLAYTON DINGLE
GAVE YOU A SENSE OF ADVENTURE AND A TINGLE
AS SECRETLY READING THE 'REVEILLE'
UNDER A BLANKET AT NIGHT - WITH A FLASHLIGHT

"GORRA MATCH?" - "YEH! YOUR FACE AN MY ARSE!"
LIGHTING FARTS - WHOOOSH! WHAT A FARCE
SMOKIN' DIMPS "GIVE US A DRAG - DRY LIPS - NO DUCKS ARSE!"

AFTER THE TRUE DARE, KISS, COMMAND & PROMISE &
"O'GRADY SAY'S DO THIS - O'GRADY SAY'S DO THAT" GAMES

THE POET LAUREATE OF THE GANG
WHO ACCLAIMED TO BEING QUITE WITTY
WOULD RECITE US HIS FAMOUS WINDBREAKIN' LITTLE DITTY -

"A FART IS A SLIGHT EXPLOSION
IT COMES FROM THE PLANET BUM
SAILS THROUGH THE VALLEY OF TROUSERS
AND COMES OUT WITH A SLIGHT HUM."

FOLLOWED BY AN ODE TO THE LOCAL BAKERY –
"DON'T EAT PRICE'S BREAD, DON'T EAT PRICE'S BREAD
IT MAKES YOU SH*T THE BED
NO BLOODY WONDER YOU FART LIKE THUNDER
DON'T EAT PRICE'S BREAD."

THEN CAME THE OBSCENE "THE BOY STOOD ON THE BURNING DECK,"
FOLLOWED BY "GOOD JESUS MR. MURPHY,
GOD BLESS YOUR HEART & SOUL,"

AND FINISHED WITH THE MOST OBSCENE OF ALL –
"THREE GERMAN OFFICERS CROSSED THE LINE TABOO! TABOO!"

"WHO'S KNITTED YOUR FACE AND DROPPED A STITCH?"
SCOWLED A PASSING LITTLE TITCH

"CHEWIN' A BRICK OR WHAT?" CAME THE WITTY RETORT
"STICKS & STONES WILL BREAK MY BONES
BUT NAMES WILL NEVER HURT ME."

"HUH! DO YOU WANNA 'CLAYTON KISS' – YAH! CHEEKY YOUNG PUP?"
"NERR! YOU CAN'T STICK ONE ON ME –
'COS I'VE GOT MI BALLIES UP!"

THEN MISBEHAVING WITH A MAGNIFYING GLASS –
BY TOYING WITH A SHAFT OF SUNLIGHT
ONTO A NEWSPAPER 'TIL IT SET ALIGHT
OR THE BACK OF YOUR VICTIM'S HAND 'TIL' IT SCORCHED
AND GAVE HIM A TERRIBLE FRIGHT-YYYEEOW!

LAYING A PENNY COIN ON A TRAIN LINE
MAKING IT EXPAND, GLEAM AND SHINE

MUM AND GRAN WOULD SIT KNITTING BY THE BLAZING FIRESIDE
FRANTICALLY SUCKING 'UNCLE JOE'S MINTBALLS'
WITH THEIR 'CORNED BEEF LIKE LEGS' GLOWING IN THE DARK

FOLLOWED BY THE RITUAL
OF COUNTING AND CALCULATING THEIR
GREENSHIELD STAMPS & BLACK AND GREENS TEA COUPONS
BY THE BUNDLE WHILE US KIDS WOULD TRUNDLE

OFF TO THE LOCAL CORNER SHOP TO TAKE THE EMPTIES BACK
CORONA AND TIZER MINERAL BOTTLES FOR THREPENCE A THROW
THEN OFF OUT TO CLAYTON PARK WE'D GO

I RECALL US SCALLIES SWIPING A COUPLE OF CRATES OF 'TIZER'

BIG MINERAL BOTTLES FROM THE BACKYARD
OF THE LOCAL CORNER TOFFEE SHOP
WHERE THEY USED TO STACK THEM - WHAT LUCK!

WE STASHED THEM BEHIND SOME DERELICT GARAGES ACROSS THE WAY
- WE NEVER WENT THIRSTY FOR A YEAR AND A DAY
(AND WE EVEN TOOK THE EMPTIES BACK - WHAT CHEEK!)

SOMETIMES WE'D NAUGHTILY RAID OUR MONEY BOXES
AND BUY 5 WOODBINES OR 10 PARK DRIVE TIPPED CIGGIES
& A PACKET OF POLO MINTS (TO TAKE THE SMELL OF SMOKE AWAY)

A PACKET OF SPANGLES,
A PENDLETONS TWICER -
NOTHING NICER!
AND A FROZEN JUBBLY
- EEH! IT WERE LUBBLY!

THEN WE'D GO OFF HUNTING
FOR OUR FRIDAY NIGHT PREY
THE LOCAL FLICKS

'THE CARLTON' IN CLAYTON
'THE NEW ROYAL' IN BRADFORD
'THE MOKO' (THE MOSELY) OR 'THE DON' IN BESWICK
- WHERE WE'D GET UP TO OUR TEENAGE BOYISH TRICKS

LIKE SITTING NEXT TO YOUR CHOSEN TARGET
AND PRETEND TO YAWN
ARM CASUALLY OUTSTRETCHED
AND SEDUCTIVELY LANDING OVER
HER FROZEN WITH FEAR, TREMBLING SHOULDER

THEN TRYING IN VAIN TO KISS HER
ON THOSE RUBY RED LIPSTICK LIPS
SOMETIMES YOU'D CLICK
BUT MOST TIMES WITH DEFIANCE
YOUR ARM WOULD RAPIDLY RETURN WITH A VENGEANCE

ALSO PULLING THEIR HAIR FROM BEHIND
WAS MAYBE A BIT PATHETIC & SAD
AS YOU INVARIABLY ENDED UP WITH AN ICE-CREAM CORNET
STUCK ON TOP OF YOUR BIG DAFT HEAD……

RAVENSBURY F.C. (1963)

PLAYING WITH PRIDE FOR OUR SCHOOL FOOTBALL TEAM
WAS A DREAM COME TRUE
I EVEN SCORED IN THE FIRST 3 MIN'S OF MY DEBUT
IN WHICH WE LOST 7 - 2

AFTER A SUCCESSION OF HEAVY DEFEATS
WE WERE TAKEN UNDER THE WING OF OUR DEPUTY HEAD
AND SCIENCE TEACHER MR. (TED) REARDON
WHO TRANSFORMED US INTO A CHAMPIONSHIP WINNING SIDE

WE ALWAYS PLAYED IN SLUTCH AND MUD
(DUE TO OUR NORTH WEST WEATHER)
ON THE JOHNSON & HEWLETT PLAYING FIELDS
OR ON THE 'RED REC' (RED SHALE) ASHTON NEW ROAD
EVEN WORSE ON THAT 'BLACK SHINGLE' - ON CLAYTON DINGLE

I REMEMBER THAT HEAVY LEADENED LEATHER CASEY
WHICH WEIGHED AN ABSOLUTE TON
WHEN IT GOT SOAKED IN MUD AND SHIT
IT WAS LIKE A MEDICINE BALL
AND YOU WOULD DO A SPECTACULAR SCISSOR OR OVERHEAD KICK
- JUST TO AVOID HEADING IT!

SOMETIMES IT KIND OF HIT YOU ON THE HEAD
LEAVING YOU HALF CONSCIOUS
WITH ITS LACE EMBEDDED IN YOUR FOREHEAD

THAT FEELING I'LL NEVER FORGET
WHEN WALKIN' DOWN OUR STREET IN MUD ABSOLUTELY SOAKIN' WET
HAVING SCORED A 'HAT TRICK' - WAS JUST TERRIFIC!

THE STARS WHO PLAYED FOR 'RAVEY' SUPER WHITES WERE -
IN GOALS - BRIAN (HOBBO) HOBSON
FULL BACKS - PETE (MO) TRINNICK, CLIVE STOCKWELL,
DAVE (ROBBO) ROBINSON & DENIS WILSON
HALF BACKS - CLIFF (RAMMA) ROBERTS,
DAVE (MAC) MCLOUGHLIN & JOHNNY WHISKER
WINGERS - GEOFF HALL, STEVE (PIGGY) SMITH,
PHIL PRESTBURY, COLIN (SLASH) ASHTON
FORWARDS - MIKE BALL, DAVE (PRESS) PRESTBURY, BILLY HALL
ROB (NOBBY) HUGHES (OUR CAPTAIN) & GED (EDDER) PLATT

THREE OF OUR LADS WERE OUTSTANDING -
GED PLATT & GEOFF HALL PLAYED FOR EAST MANCHESTER AREA TEAM
NOBBY HUGHES COULD HAVE PLAYED FOR MANCHESTER BOYS
IF HE HAD STAYED ON AT SCHOOL BUT HE DECLINED
AND LEFT TO SERVE HIS TIME......

CAPT. 'NOBBY' HUGHES
WITH TEAM MANAGER &
DEPUTY HEADMASTER
'TED REARDON'

SCHOOL CRICKET TEAM

WAS MOSTLY THE FOOTBALL TEAM IN DISGUISE
WE PLAYED MANY OF OUR MATCHES ON THE INFAMOUS 'RED REC'
THE BEST CRICKETERS WERE THE BEST FOOTBALLERS
GED 'POWERHOUSE' PLATT & NOBBY 'SLOGGER' HUGHES

WHO HIT A SIX ONE DAY -
RIGHT THROUGH 'STOKES'S' CAKE SHOP WINDOW - ACROSS THE WAY
(MIND YOU THEIR 'ROCK CAKES' WERE AS HARD AS ANY CORKY BALL)

MY BRUV PHIL WAS ALSO AN EXCELLENT LEFT HANDED BATSMAN
WHO GAVE IT A GOOD CLOUT AND AN EVEN BETTER FIELDER -
WITH A SUPERB ACCURATE THROW - THAT GOT MANY A RUN OUT

ACE BOWLERS BRIAN HOBSON (HOBBO) AND GEOFF HALL -
THEY WERE WIZARDS WITH THAT CORKY BALL......

RUGGER

AFTER FALLING OUT WITH OUR FOOTBALL TEAM
FOR BEING DROPPED FOR A LESSER PLAYER - I MEAN!
I JOINED THE SCHOOL RUGBY UNION TEAM

PLAYED WING THREE QUARTERS AND SOMETIMES IN THE SCRUM
I DIDN'T SEEM TO DO MUCH
APART FROM HOOFIN' THE BALL OUT OF TOUCH
OR GO ON AN OCCASIONAL JINKING TYPE RUN

I REMEMBER SCORING A SENSATIONAL TRY ONCE
PLAYING AGAINST LADYBARN SCHOOL (WYTHENSHAWE)

THEY HAD THIS GREAT FLOWING ALL PROFESSIONAL
LIKE PASSING MOVEMENT
& I CLOCKED IT, HUNG BACK, THEN RAN LIKE A BAT OUT OF HELL
AS THEY WERE ABOUT TO PASS THE BALL -
CAUGHT IT - AND RAN ABOUT A MILLION MILES AN HOUR
OVER THAT WILD, WET AND WINDY PITCH -
LIKE A FART WITH GOLLIES ON! - OUT OF SHEER FEAR
(AFTER SEEING THE SIZE OF GUYS CHASING AFTER MI BLOOD)

AND TOUCHED DOWN - TO A FAINT CHEER!
WITH ABOUT TEN GORILLA SIZED GUYS LANDING ON TOP OF ME
I WAS SPLATTERED, PULVERIZED & EMBEDDED DEEP IN THE MUD.....

TAKEN FOR A RIDE

DOWN THROUGH THE STREETS I'D PEDDLE
ON MY 'SECOND HAND' SUNBEAM RAPIER BICYCLE
OVER THOSE 'CRUSTY LOAF' LIKE COBBLE STONES
BUMP! BUMP! BUMP! MY BUM WENT LIKE THE CLAPPERS
ON THAT EVER SO SORE SADDLE & OH! MY POOR ACHIN' BONES
SOMETIMES I WOULD RIDE ON MY MATE EDDY'S TANDEM
HIM PEDDLING FURIOUSLY AT THE FRONT –
ME WITH MY LAZY FEET RESTING ON THE FRAME AT THE REAR AT RANDOM
"ARE YOU PEDDLIN' PRESS?"
HE'D SHOUT SWEATING, SWEARING & PANTING PROFUMIOUSLY
"COURSE I AM", LIES I, SNIGGERING MISCHIEVIOUSLY
AS WE CYCLED ON INTO THE COUNTRYSIDE
& THE QUESTION WAS – WHO WAS TAKING WHO FOR A RIDE?......

THE CUT (CANAL)

WITH WINDBLOWN WINDJAMMERS, WE COVORTED MENACINGLY BY THE 'CUT'
BALANCING DARINGLY ON THOSE GIANT WOODEN WET SODDEN LOCKS
SCAMPERING ALONG THE SLUICE GATES WITH WET SHOES AND SOCKS
MADLY ATTEMPTING TO JUMP THE WIDTH OF THE CUT
SOMETIMES FALLING BACKWARDS INTO THAT GRIMY GREEN WATER
THAT WAS LITTERED WITH 'OL BIKEFRAMES, LICHEN AND LEECHES
WWHOA! HHELP! ARRRGH! SPLUT!!......

DAISY NOOK FAIR (FAILSWORTH)

EVERY EASTER WE WOULD TRUNDLE OFF TO DAISY NOOK ANNUAL FAIR
GOING FIRST ON THAT GGGGGHOST TRAIN FOR A SCARE
ONTO THE WHIRLING WALZER AND WALL-OF-DEATH RIDE
THAT GAVE YOU THE SHITS

INTO THE FUN HOUSE WITH THOSE DISTORTED MIRRORS
AND ROTATING BARREL OF LAUGHS THAT HAD YOU IN FITS
SLAMMIN' & RAMMIN' ON THOSE DAREDEVIL DODGEMS WHAT A SHOUT
BACK ONTO THE MERRY-GO-ROUND AND UP-AND-DOWN ROUNDABOUT
STANDING UP ON THE BIG WHEEL MAKIN' THE LITTLE GIRLS SQUEAL

RIDING THE SCENIC RAILWAY AND THAT SEA SICK SWINGBOAT
SLIDING DOWN THE SHUTE ON THE HELTER SKELTER
HEADLONG INTO THE GROUND - WAS SOUND

THEN OVER TO THOSE SEEDY SIDE STALLS -
THE RIFLE RANGE AND TRY-YOUR-STRENGTH-MACHINE
ROLL A PENNY 'TIL YOU HAVEN'T ANY
HOOK A DUCK - STILL NO LUCK!

LOBBIN' BEAN BAGS AT THE COCONUT SHYS
HURLIN' HOOPS, CHUCKIN' THOSE (WEIGHTED) DARTS
AND SURPRISE, SURPRISE - YOU'VE WON A PRIZE!
A WINDMILL ON A STICK - A GOLDFISH
SCOFFIN' TOFFEE APPLES, CANDY FLOSS AND SUGAR DUMMIES
HOT DOGS, ICE CREAM, CHIPS AND FISH

LISTENING TO THE BEATLES 'GIVE ME MONEY'
THE HOLLIES 'ON A CAROUSEL' AND THE SEARCHERS
'SWEETS FOR MY SWEET - SUGAR FOR MY HONEY'
AND IF YOU LEFT THE SIDE STALLS
WITH A GOLDFISH IN ONE HAND AND A COCONUT IN THE OTHER -
YOU'D BE CHUFFED TO LITTLE MINT BALLS ......

FROM A JACK TO A KING

FRIDAY NIGHTS AFTER SCHOOL
OUR GANG OF FIFTEEN YEAR OLDS
WOULD CONGREGATE AT 'KNOX'S CAFE' FAIRFIELD, DROYLSDEN
WHERE THEY HAD THIS WONDERFUL 'WURLITZER' JUKE BOX
THAT PLAYED ALL OUR FAVOURITE 45'S

WE'D SIT THERE SUPPIN' HOT EXPRESSO COFFEE
AND ICE COLD MILK SHAKES
OCCASIONALLY WE'D GET UP TO JIVE
WITH THE LOCAL BINTS WITH THE BACKCOMBED BEEHIVES

EVERY SO OFTEN YOU'D GET THE ODD IRATE TEDDY BOY
WHO'D THREATEN US YOUNG TEENIES WITH EXTREME VIOLENCE
SOMETIMES FLICK-KNIVES WOULD APPEAR
AND WE'D ALL PANIC AND SCARPER OUT OF FEAR

I REMEMBER US TEENIES BEING CHASED ONE NIGHT
RUNNING FAST AND FURIOUS, DOWN THE STREETS AND BACK ENTRIES
WHERE I STOPPED AND CLAMBERED OVER A BACKYARD GATE
HIDING THERE, GASPING FOR BREATH AND OUT OF SIGHT
PHEW! UNTIL THEY ALL RAN PASSED

HOLDING MY BREATH AND SNIGGERING OUT OF EXCITEMENT AND FEAR
I THEN JUMPED BACK OVER THE GATE
CASUALLY COMBED MY QUIFF AND D.A. (STILL NO SIDEBURNS?)
AND STROLLED BOWLEGGED TO MY LAIR

APTLY SINGING THAT GOOD OL' ROCK AND ROLL SONG
BY JOHNNY KIDD & THE PIRATES -
"SHIVERS DOWN MY BACKBONE
I GOT THE SHAKES IN THE THIGH BONE
SHIVERS IN MY KNEE BONE - SSSHAKIN' ALL OVERRRR"

THEN I'D CARRY ON WHISTLING AND SINGING
THAT NED MILLER SONG -
"FROM A JACK TO A KING OF LONELINESS
TO A WEDDING, WEDDING, WEDDING RING
I PLAYED AN ACE AND WON THE QUEEN
YOU MADE ME KING OF YOUR HEART".....

STAYING AT GRANDMA'S

ALONE IN MY BED AT NIGHT, OUTSIDE THE BEDROOM WINDOW
THAT DIM, YELLOWING STREET LAMP
WOULD CAST DARK, EERIE, NIGHTMARISH SHADOWS
THROUGH THE ALMOST THREADBARE CURTAINS
ONTO THE SILENT CEILING - MY IMAGINATION WAS REELING
AS I HALF SCARED MYSELF TO SLEEP, GOING UNDERCOVER,
FEELING WARM AND PROTECTED, I DAREN'T PEEP

I AWOKE THE FROST FREEZING MORNING
ALMOST KICKED OVER THE 'GUZZUNDER' (GERRY) STILL HALF DOPED
AS I SCURRIED INTO THAT ICE COLD BATHROOM
THAT SMELT STRONGLY OF PEARS SOAP
HAD A COLD RINSE, A PEE, BRUSHED MY TEETH AND HAIR

DOWN THE STEEP STAIRS INTO THE BEST CHAIR
FOR A NICE CUP OF GRANDMA'S 'ROSIE LEE' (TEA)
FOLLOWED BY A PIPIN' HOT BOWL OF SCOTCH PORRIDGE OATS
AS I STARED WIDE-EYED INTO THAT BLAZING HOT FLICKERING FIRE

"MORNING!" I MUTTERED, AS GRANDMA TUNED IN THE RADIO
TO THE 'BILLY COTTON BAND SHOW' - "WAKEY! WAAAAKAAAY!"
"MORNIN'!" GRUMPED GRANDAD, HIS FADING SANDY HAIR,
RUST RED WAISTCOAT WITH POCKET WATCH COMPLETE,
ARMBANDS HOLDING UP HIS YELLOWING STRIPED COLLARLESS SHIRT,
HIS INCESSANT SNIFFING AND SPLUTTERING
ON HIS 'WILLS WILD WOODBINES' - HE LOOKED BEAT

WATCHING GRANDMA BUTTERING TOAST
HER SNOW WHITE COTTON WOOL HAIR FLOWING - THE PERFECT HOST
"I'VE MADE US SOME COCONUT CAKE FOR LATER" SHE WOULD BOAST
"NOW HERE YOUNG UN' HAVE A NICE PIECE OF TOAST"

THE MIXED AROMA OF TOAST, LAVENDER
& STALE TOBACCO CONSUMED THE AIR

"I MUST GERROFF TO DO MI PAPER ROUND GRANDMA" I'D DECLARE
"IT'S A BIT FOGGY OUT THERE" GRUMBLED GRANDAD
AS I SLIPPED ON MY GREY CANVAS PAPERBAG, STILL YYYAWWWNING!
"SEE YOU LATER GRAN," - "GOODBYE AND TAKE CARE!" SHE'D SAY
THEN WAVE ME OFF DOWN THE STREET UNTIL I'D DISAPPEAR
INTO THAT 'THICK AS PEA SOUP' FREEZING, FOGGY AIR……

LEAVING SCHOOL

WINTER CAME WITH A VENGEANCE IN '63
WHICH WAS UNFORTUNATE YOU SEE
'COS ONE OF THOSE FROST-BITTEN AND CHERRY-NOSED PAPERBOYS
THAT WAS FROZEN TO TH'BONE THAT SEVERE WINTER - WAS ME!

1963 WAS THE YEAR OF 'THE GREAT TRAIN ROBBERY'
IT WAS ALSO THE YEAR OF THE 'PROFUMO SCANDAL'
INVOLVING CALL GIRLS 'CHRISTINE KEELER'
AND 'MANDY RICE-DAVIES' THAT SHOOK PARLIMENT
& LED TO THE DOWNFALL OF THE 'McMILLAN' TORY GOVERNMENT

'J.F.KENNEDY' THE AMERICAN PRESIDENT
WAS ASSASSINATED ON THE STREETS OF DALLAS
BY HIT MAN 'LEE HARVEY OSWALD'
BUT MOST IMPORTANT OF ALL - IT WAS THE YEAR I LEFT SCHOOL

LEAVING SCHOOL AND FEELING GRAND
EXCHANGIN' YOUR OL' SCHOOL SATCHEL
FOR A 'VIRGIN' TOOL BAG IN YOUR EAGER HAND
AN APPRENTICE COMPOSITOR I WAS TO BE
ON £3.00 PER WEEK - WHAT A SALARY!

IN FACT, I USED TO GO CLUBBING ALMOST
EVERY FRI, SAT & SUN NIGHTS
TO THOSE COFFEE BAR CLUBS -
'OASIS' & 'THE TWISTED WHEEL'- TOO YOUNG FOR PUBS!

I WORKED FOR A SMALL LETTERPRESS PRINTERS
CALLED 'RIMSON LTD.' IN HOULDSWORTH STREET,
NEAR THE CITY CENTRE, IT WAS A NINE TO FIVE JOB

ALTHOUGH I USED TO ARRIVE FOR WORK ABOUT 9.50 a.m.
10 MINS. BEFORE OUR BOSS, WHO ALWAYS ARRIVED AT 10.00 a.m.
ON THE ODD OCCASION HE WOULD COME IN EARLY
- CATCH ME AND GIVE ME A RIGHT OL' ROLLOCKIN'

SKIVVING ON THE TOILET AND HAVING A SLY FAG
READING AN 'HANK JANSEN' BOOK OR A 'PARADE' GIRLY MAG.
"HAVE YOU FALLEN DOWN?"
"SHOUTED OUR GRUMPY 'OL GIT OF A BOSS, WITH A FROWN

"COMIN'! JUST FINISHIN'!"- AS I PRETENDED TO WIPE MY BUM
ON LAST NIGHT'S 'EVENING CHRON'
OR A TELEPHONE DIRECTORY CUT TO HALF SIZE
THAT ALWAYS BROUGHT TEARS TO YOUR EYES

GOING FOR CHIPPY DINNERS & MAKIN' BREWS
WAS MY EXPECTED APPRENTICE CHORES
WE HAD AN OL' WOODEN BENCH WITH A SLOP BOARD
& A LITTLE ELECTRIC OVEN WE BAKED JACKET SPUDS IN

GARNISHED WITH ECHO MARGARINE –
A CHEAP MEAL FOR US UNDERPAID COMP'S
THAT WAS GRACIOUSLY DIGESTED
BUT NOT FOR OUR STINGY BOSS IT MUST HAVE COST HIM
AN ARM & A LEG AS HIS INFLATED ELECTRIC BILL SUGGESTED

ONE HEADY WEEKEND UNBEKNOWN TO OUR BOSS –
I ONCE AQUIRED THE KEYS & OPENED THE FACTORY WORKSHOP
– TO DO A FOREIGNER – 'WEDDING INVITATIONS CARDS'
AS WE NEVER WORKED WEEKENDS

THERE I WAS SNEAKILY PRINTING THE INVITATIONS
WHEN THE DOORBELL RANG – I FROZE WITH FRIGHT
IT WAS THE OL' GUY BILL, FROM THE CORNER NEWSAGENTS SHOP
TO LET ME KNOW THAT HE KNEW WHAT I WAS UP TOO

IT TAUGHT ME A LESSON, IT WAS A BLESSIN'
(AND HE NEVER GRASSED ME UP – GOD BLESS HIM)

PLAYING PUSH H'PENNY AT DINNER TIMES
WAS DEADLY SERIOUS STUFF
THE GAME WAS FIERCLY FOUGHT AS IF OUR LIVES DEPENDED ON IT
& ME BEING THE YOUNGEST – WAS NEVER ALLOWED TO WIN
– IT WAS A CARDINAL SIN

AT 'RADIO RIMSONS', I USED TO PLAY HOUSE D.J.
ON MY OL' DANSETTE
AND SPEND HOURS ON THE PHONE TO MY GIRLFRIENDS
HAVING A GOOD OL' TEENAGE CHIT CHAT

MY WORK MATES AT RIMSONS WERE – ROY 'THE BOY' CONNOR
WHO SUPPORTED AN ARMY TYPE 'SHORT BACK & SIDES' HAIRCUT
A BIT OF A 'SQUARE' & ALWAYS WORE BRACES
HE USED TO TELL ME OL' ARMY STORIES THAT FASCINATED ME
& JOKES BY THE BUCKET LOADS THAT HAD ME IN STITCHES

& PHIL CHADWICK – AN AVID BUDDY HOLLY & EDDY COCHRAN FAN
WITH HIS ROCK & ROLL GOOD LOOKS & EVIS QUIFF
HE WOULD LEAN & LETCH OUT OF THE WORKS WINDOW

& WAVE AT THE PRETTY YOUNG 'BITS OF FLUFF' THAT PASSED BY
TO CATCH THEIR TWINKLIN' EYE & A FLASH OF BARE THIGH

I REMEMBER HAVING THE HOTS FOR THIS
GORGEOUS RAVEN HAIRED BEAUTY
WHO PASSED BY EACH DAY, ON HER WAY
TO SMITHFIELD MARKET OFFICES

UNTIL I FOUND OUT MONTHS LATER
THAT SHE WAS ACTUALLY MY COUSIN IRENE
- WHICH SEEMED KIND OF WEIRD

ALSO REMEMBER WHEN I WAS A VIRGINAL SIXTEEN YEAR OLD
& FLUFFED MY CHANCE, PATHETICALLY TO 'PEEL MY PLUMB'
WITH MY GIRLFRIEND 'BABS', ON CLAYTON DINGLE

- COS I COULDN'T GET HER SUSSY'S OFF
THUS GAVE UP MISERABLY & DEJECTEDLY

- WELL MY MATE 'SEX-STARVED' PHIL WHO WAS EIGHTEEN
KNOCKED ME ALL OVER THE PLACE
FOR MISSING MY GOLDEN OPPORTUNITY –
MY FIRST LAY & BEING AN ABSOLUTE DISGRACE!

HE ACTUALLY DREW ME A DIAGRAM OF HOW
TO UNCLIP A SUSPENDER BELT
THUS REMOVING THE OFFENDING OBSTACLE
- FOR ANY FUTURE CONQUESTS THAT CAME MY WAY

I LOVED GOING OUT & ABOUT THE TOWN CENTRE
DELIVERING INVOICES & COLLECTING PATTERN CARD SAMPLES
FROM THE TEXTILE MANUFACTURERS WE PRINTED FOR

PLUS DELIVERING PRINTED INVITATIONS & MENU CARDS FOR
THE MANCHESTER & SALFORD MASONIC HALLS
AND SOMEHOW I ALWAYS SEEMED TO ARRIVE BACK
AT NOTABLE 'BREW TIMES' BETWEEN CALLS

1963 WAS THE YEAR MAN. UNITED WON THE F.A. CUP
3 - 1 AGAINST FAVOURITES LEICESTER CITY AT WEMBLEY
DAY'S OF DENIS LAW, BOBBY CHARLTON, DAVID HERD,
ALBERT QUIXALL, PADDY CRERAND, BILLY FOULKES
THE FOUNDATION OF THE GREAT 60'S TEAM THAT WAS TO BE

ALSO IT WAS THE CHILLING YEAR OF THE 'MOORS MURDERS'
THAT SENT SHIVERS DOWN OUR SPINES
I ATTENDED A DOUBLE WEDDING OF MY TWO COUSINS FROM GORTON
ON THE VERY DAY AFTER 'PAULINE READ' HAD GONE MISSING
HER PARENTS WERE AT THIS WEDDING & WORRIED SICK
THIS WAS BEFORE IT ALL CAME OUT - IT WAS UNCANNY

IT HIT EVERBODY HARD, 'BRADY & HINDLEY'
WERE PYCHOS - IT WAS BEYOND BELIEF
HOW THEY KIDNAPPED & SADISTICALLY TORTURED
THOSE POOR LITTLE SOULS,
ABSOLUTELY SICK, HARROWING & HORRIFIC
& IT HAPPENED IN OUR OWN BACKYARD....

MY COUSINS (SISTERS LILLIAN & JEAN) DOUBLE WEDDING
(WITH THEIR NEW HUSBANDS BERNARD & BRIAN)
AT GORTON MONASTERY

COUSIN IRENE SECOND FROM THE RIGHT

SWEET SIXTEEN (A LOST OPPORTUNITY!)

WOOED MY LOVER TO CLAYTON DINGLE
LAID HER DOWN ON SHALE & SHINGLE
WE SLAPPED AN' TICKLED, FRENCH KISSED AN' GIGGLED
WE UNZIPPED, UNHOOKED, FONDLED AN' FIDDLED
THEN SHE HITCHED UP HER SKIRT & GAVE OUT A SIGH!
REVEALING FISHNET STOCKINGS, SUSPENDERS
- PLUS THAT PATCH OF BARE THIGH!

BENEATH THE STARRY SKY & SHIMMERING MOON
I RANTED & GRUNTED LIKE A RAMPANT BABOON
AS SHE WHISTLED THE LATEST BEATLES TUNE -

READY FOR ACTION - WE LAY BACK IN AWE
I RIPPED OFF MY SHIRT & STRIPPED TO THE RAW
I TUGGED AN' I PULLED I SWEATED AN' CURSED
SHE JUST TWIDDLED HER TOES AN' SAID "AM I YOUR FIRST?"

"YYYESS!!" SAY'S I - SO EMBARRASSED I FELT
COS I COULN'T GET OFF HER BLEEDIN' SUSPENDER BELT
"TUTT! TUTT!" - SHE TUTTED, SHOOK HER HEAD WITH DEPAIR
STRAIGHTENED HER SKIRT AND TIDIED HER HAIR
"CALLOW YOUNG FELLOW IT'S EXPERIENCE YOU LACK!" "OH! YEH!
WELL!" I RETORTED "AT LEAST MY VIRGINITY'S INTACT!!"

RHYTHM & BLUES

BEING A TEAR-ARSED TEENAGER IN 1963 WAS A HIGH ON A HIGH
AS JIMMY HENDRIX LATER SANG "EXCUSE ME WHILE I KISS THE SKY"
IT WAS AFTER THE LULL IN THE EARLY SIXTIES

APART FROM ELVIS, CLIFF & THE SHAD'S,
BUDDY HOLLY, DEL SHANNON, THE EVERLY'S & THE BIG 'O'
THE NEW MUSIC HAD ARRIVED -

'RHYTHM & BLUES' HAD PRECEDED 'ROCK & ROLL'
THE WHOLE COUNTRY WAS BUZZING - MODS VERSUS ROCKERS
MODS 'HIPPY HIPPY SHAKED'- WHERE THE TEDS ONCE JIVED

BEATLE FLOP TOP HAIR STYLES DID AWAY
WITH THAT BRYLCREMED QUIFF & D.A. (DUCKS ARSE)
(ALSO THOSE LITTLE BRYLCREEM MACHINES WE HAD IN THE LOCAL
SWIMMING BATHS-THAT GAVE YOU A LITTLE BLOB FOR A TANNER)

REMEMBER THOSE RIBBED KNITTED SWIMMING TRUNKS THAT GOT SO
SODDEN YOUR GUSSET WENT DOWN TO YOUR ANKLES & EXPOSED YOUR
SHRIVELLED UP LITTLE WILLY MAKING YOU LOOK REALLY SILLY

BEATLE CUT AWAY COLLAR 'PIERRE CARDIN' SUITS
REPLACED THOSE EDWARDIAN 'MONKEY SUITS'
CUBAN HEELS AND CHELSEA BOOTS WERE IN -

KICKING THOSE CREPE-SOLED 'BROTHEL CREEPERS' OUT
AND 'FLARES' FLUSHED THOSE 'DRAINPIPES' DOWN THE SPOUT
THE 'ELVIS' SNEER WAS SUBSTITUTED FOR THE 'MICK JAGGER' POUT

PIRATE RADIO STATIONS
LIKE 'RADIO CAROLINE'
TOOK OVER FROM THAT CRACKLY
'RADIO LUXENBURG'
WITH PIRATE D.J.'s JOHN PEEL,
TONY BLACKBURN, KENNY EVERET,
ED 'STEWPOT' AND SIMON DEE

WHICH YOU TUNED IN TO ON
YOUR NEW 'TRANNY'
(TRANSISTOR RADIO IN A
LITTLE LEATHER CASE)
PURCHASED FROM 'MAZEL RADIO'
ON LONDON ROAD,
AND IF YOU WERE FEELING FLUSHED WITH
EXTRA DOSH YOU COULD BUY
EX-JUKE BOX 45's BY THE DOZ.

MAZEL'S USED TO SELL ALL KINDS OF ELECTRICAL SPARES LIKE
OLD T.V. VALVES,SECOND HAND DANSETTES, OLD MAINS RADIOS
PLUS LOTS & LOTS OF ITEMS IN BIG HEAPS EVERWHERE

THOSE MUSIC SHOPS LIKE 'RENOS', 'MAMELOKS',
'FORSYTHS' AND 'JOHNNY ROADHOUSE'S' (FROM THE N.D.O.)
THAT SOLD ALL KINDS OF MUSICAL INSTRUMENTS -
GUITARS, HARMONICAS, TAMBOURINES, MARACCAS
PIANOS & PREMIER DRUM KITS

FOR ALL THE BUDDING LOCAL GROUPS LIKE 'THE HOLLIES',
'WAYNE BANANA (FONTANA)' AND 'HERMAN' HERMITS'
& THE REST OF US SPOTTY LITTLE HERBERTS......

'ELVIS' PRESTBURY'

THE OASIS

WAS ONE OF THOSE SMOKEY, SEEDY, CELLAR CLUBS OF THE SIXTIES
WITH CONDENSATION DRIPPING OFF
THOSE DARK, DANK, ROUGH AND RED BRICKED WALLS
FLOURESCENT U.V. LAMPS THAT USED TO SHOW UP DANDRUFF
ON YOUR COLLAR AND GAVE YOU GRIEF
ESPECIALLY IF YOU HAD A FALSE TOOTH –
IT WOULD SHOW UP DARK - CONTRASTING WITH THOSE PEARLY WHITE TEETH

"LEMME TELL YA 'BOUT A GIRL I KNOW – I'M TALKIN'
'BOUT YOU' NOBODY BUT YOU"
"WALKIN' THE DOG J J J J J JUSTA WALKIN"
OR "I'M A HOG FOR YA BABY, CAN'T GERRA 'NOUGH OF YER LURVVE"
ALWAYS STARTED THE SETS AND THEY ALWAYS FINISHED OFF WITH
"TOO MUCH MONKEY BUSINESS" OR "GIMME MONEY THAT'SSS WOR I WANT"
(AND ALL THE GROUPS SEEMED TO SING WITH FALSE SCOUSE ACCENTS!)

HOUSE D.J. WAS A CHARACTER CALLED 'MAC MAGONEGALL LACEY'
HE WAS A REALLY CHEESY AND CORNY GUY WHO USED TO SHOUT
"SHAKE IT UP NOW!" (EVERY TEN SECONDS!) AND PLAY INCESSANTLY
LITTLE STEVIE WONDER'S' –"FINGERTIPS PART ONE & PART TWO"

WE'D ALL CRINGE & SQUIRM
'COS HE SEEMED SO FAKE!

THE OASIS WAS OWNED
BY TOP JAZZ MUSICIAN
'TONY STUART'
& HAD THREE STAGES
ONE SET AFTER ANOTHER
THE GROUPS APPEARED
AS WE DANCED TO
THE 'MASHED POTATO',
THE 'CAVERN STOMP',
'RINGO'S DOG' AND THAT
KNEE JERKIN' 'HIPPY,
HIPPY, SHAKE'......

MY MEMBERSHIP CARD 1963

45-47 LLOYD ST
MANCHESTER 2
BLA 6363

GROUPS (THAT APPEARED AT THE OASIS)

PETE MACLAINE & THE CLAN, JOHNNY PETERS & THE CRESTAS
LORRAINE GRAY & THE CHAPERONES, MIKE CADILLAC & THE PLAYBOYS
THE MARAUDERS - 'THAT'S WHAT I WANT'
IVAN'S MEADS, THE COUNTRY GENTS - 'GREENSLEEVES'
THE STYLOS (WITH MIKE HARDING)
JOHNNY KIDD & THE PIRATES - 'SHAKIN' ALL OVER'

THE HOLLIES - 'SEARCHIN' & 'JUST ONE LOOK'
HERMAN'S HERMITS - 'I'M INTO SOMETHING GOOD'
DAVE BERRY & THE CRUISERS - 'MEMPHIS TENNESEE'
WAYNE FONTANA & THE MINDBENDERS - 'UM UM UM UM UM UM'
RED HOFFMAN & THE MEASLES (ENGLAND'S ANSWER TO P.J. PROBY!)
FREDDIE & THE DREAMERS - 'IF YOU'VE GOTTA MAKE A FOOL'

JOE BROWN & THE BRUVVERS - 'A PICTURE OF YOU'
GOLDIE & THE GINGERBREADS - 'CAN'T YOU HEAR MY HEARTBEAT'
MILLIE - 'MY BOY LOLLIPOP'
THE TOGGERY FIVE, ST. LOUIS UNION - 'GIRL'
THE FOUR PENNIES - 'JULIET'
SCREAMING LORD SUCH - 'JACK THE RIPPER'

THE UNDERTAKERS - 'MASH POTATO OH! YEH!'
REV. BLACK & THE ROCKIN' VICKERS - 'SKINNY MINNY'
FRANKENSTEIN & THE MONSTERS
THE BEATLES - 'LOVE ME DO' & 'PLEASE PLEASE ME'
GERRY & THE PACEMAKERS - 'HOW DO YOU DO IT' & 'I LIKE IT'
THE SEARCHERS -'SWEETS FOR MY SWEET' & 'NEEDLES & PINS-A'

THE MERSEYBEATS - 'I THINK OF YOU'
THE SWINGING BLUE JEANS - 'THE HIPPY HIPPY SHAKE'
BILLY KRAMER & THE DAKOTAS -
'LISTEN DO YOU WANT TO KNOW A SECRET'
THE FOURMOST - 'HELLO LITTLE GIRL'
THE FORTUNES - 'HERE IT COMES AGAIN'

THE MOJOS (WITH LEWIS COLLINS) - 'EVERYTHING'S ALRIGHT'
THE BIG THREE - 'SOME OTHER GUY NOW'
KINGSIZE TAYLOR & THE DOMINOS, THE CHANTS
SHANE FENTON & THE FENTONES, FARONS FLAMINGOS,
TOMMY QUICKLEY, THE NASHVILLE TEENS - 'TOBACCO ROAD'
THE DENNISONS - 'WALKIN' THE DOG',
THE ESCORTS - 'DIZZY MISS LIZZY',

THE BRIAN AUGER TRINITY (WITH SEX GODDESS JULIE DRISCOLL)
-"WHEEL'S ON FIRE, ROLLIN' DOWN THE ROAAAD"

THE ROLLING STONES - 'COME ON' & 'WANNA BE YOUR MAN'
THEM (WITH VAN MORRISON) 'BABY PLEASE DON'T GO' & 'GLORIA'
THE ANIMALS - 'BABY LET ME TAKE YOU HOME'
& 'HOUSE OF THE RISING SUN'

THE KINKS -'YOU REALLY GOT ME', THE WHO - 'I CAN'T EXPLAIN',
MANFRED MANN - '5 4 3 2 1', THE YARBIRDS - 'FOR YOUR LOVE'
THE SPENCER DAVIES GROUP -'GIMME SOMMA LOVIN'
THE STEAM PACKET -
WITH ROD 'THE MOD' STEWART & LONG JOHN BALDRY

EVEN HAD BIG AMERICAN STARS LIKE LITTLE RICHARD &
BO DIDDLEY & WAIT FOR IT - ROLF HARRIS & THE KANGEROOS......

LITTLE RICHARD

WAYNE FONTANA?

I'LL NEVER FORGET THE DAY
WHEN WE DUPED THESE THREE
NAIVE YOUNG SISTERS
INTO THINKING THAT
ME & MY MATES
WERE ACTUALLY -

*'WAYNE FONTANA &
THE MINDBENDERS'*
(BEFORE THEY WERE FAMOUS)

WE PICKED THEM UP FROM
THEIR LOCAL MASONETTE
THEN BACK TO MY HOUSE
WHERE THEY EXCITINGLY SAT
ALL NERVOUS & GIGGLY
IN THE LIVING ROOM

WHILE WE HAD
'BAND PRACTICE'
IN THE PARLOUR
(THE BEST ROOM)

THEN WE SNEAKLY
PUT ON *WAYNE'S & CO'S*
LATEST RELEASE
'FOR YOU, FOR YOU'
ON THE DANSETTE

WE HAD A MIKE, GUITAR & PIANO THAT WE PRETENDED TO PLAY
THEN ONE DAY THE GIRLS INFORMED US THAT WE (WAYNE & CO.)
WERE ON 'THANK YOUR LUCKY STARS' NEXT SATURDAY NIGHT

AND THEY COULN'T WAIT TO SEE US (THEIR HERO'S) ON THE TELLY
WE COULD JUST IMAGINE THEIR FACES GOING ALL RED THEN WHITE
AFTER TELLIN' ALL THEIR FRIENDS & FAMILY
- WE NEVER SAW THEM AFTER THAT......

LOCAL DRUNKS

MY BROTHERS & ME
USED TO BE ENTERTAINED
BY THE 'LOCAL DRUNKS' -
IT WAS LIKE A PANTOMIME

ARGUING WITH THE LAMP POSTS
DANCING WITH THE TELEGRAPH POLES
STAGGERING & WALKIN'
AS IF ON 'HOT COALS'

WEARING 'CHESTERS' BIG RED NOSES
CAP'S BACK TO FRONT,
COAT'S INSIDE OUT
WOBBLIN' & WHISTLIN'
ALL THE WAY HOME
SH'INGING SH'ONGS LIKE -
"THE GRREEN, GRREEN GRRASH OF HOMME"

LAUGHING HYSTERICALLY
AT UNFUNNY JOKES
TOLD IN THE 'VIC' BY UNFUNNY BLOKES
TRYING PATHETICALLY TO AMUSE
WIVE'S SHOUTING VERBAL ABUSE -

"YOU'VE SPENT THE BLEEDIN' RENT!"
WAVING THE FRYING PAN WITH GROSS INTENT
STANDING THERE ALL STUPIFIED
LOOKING SO UNDIGNIFIED

"WHAT TIME YAH! CALL THIS?"
"YER DINNER'S IN THE DOG!" & "YER TEA'S IN THE BIN!
- SO BUGGER OFF 'COS YER NOT COMIN' IN!
- AN' I'LL TELL YER FER NOWT!
- YER NOT FIT TO LET OUT!"
THEN SLAMMING THE DOOR WITH HELL OF A CLOUT

"ORRR! PLEASH, SH'WEETHEART, PLEASH LET MI IN
HIC! I'VE ONLY HAD A COUPLE OR TWO (DOZEN)"
HAND ON HIS MOUTH, STEMMIN' THE SPEW

THEN THROWIN' UP ALL OVER THE WINDOW BOX
SPLASHING & SPLATTERING HIS SHOES & SOCKS
THEN SQUATTING, ASLEEP ON THE 'CARDINAL RED'
TO DOZE THE BLEARY 'BEERY' NIGHT OF DREAD.....

CHARACTERS

"TWO AND SIX A BUNCH!"
BEGGED THE BLIND FLOWER SELLER
CROUCHED ON THE CORNER OF STEVENSON SQUARE
(OUTSIDE OF 'LOUIS GROSS'S' MENSWARE)

"TWO AND SIX A BUNCH!"
HE BELLOWED INTERMITTENTLY
YEAR AFTER YEAR AFTER YEAR
UNTIL ONE DAY HE WAS NO MORE

IN THE DISTANCE YOU COULD HEAR
THE ONE ARM NEWSPAPER SELLER BAWL
"FOOTBAWLLL! FINNAAALL!"
FROM HIS PITCH SOMEWHERE NEAR THE FREE TRADE HALL

DOWN OLDHAM STREET JUST PASSING THE HOT CHESNUT SELLER
OUTSIDE C & A'S RIGHT OPPOSITE YATE'S (BOTTOM) WINE LODGE

WENT THE MECHANICAL 'MARCHIN' MAN'
GARBED IN HIS DEMOB TRENCHCOAT AND BERET
PACING UP AND DOWN AS IF PERMANENTLY ON PARADE
"LEFT RIGHT! – LEFT RIGHT!" –
LEFT RIGHT! – LEFT RIGHT – 'BOUT TURN!"

THEN THERE WAS MAD 'MANCHESTER BILL' WHO WOULD SAY –
"WAH! WHEN I WAS ON CAMPAIGN IN AFRICA
"WAH! THEY CALLED ME 'MANCHESTER BILL'
AND WHEN I'M BACK HOME THEY CALL ME 'AFRICAN BILL' WAH!"

HE SHOUTED, THEN SALUTED AND WALKED PROUDLY AWAY
SAD CHARACTERS OF THE CITY – YOU HAD TO PITY

MORE LOCAL – YOU HAD TOOTHLESS TOMMY 'GUMMY' HOWARD
WHO ALWAYS WORE AN ARMY TUNIC AND JODPURS
ACCOMPANIED BY HIS TWO SNARLING, SPITTING ALSATION DOGS
HE WAS A NIGHTWATCHMAN AT A LOCAL SCRAPYARD

THEN THERE WAS AN EX-R.A.F. LAD CALLED FRANK
WHO USED TO STAND ON HIS HEAD
AND STARE WIDEYED, LOOKING BLANK AND STUPIFIED
AT THE FAST REVOLVING ROUNDABOUT

AND HANG UPSIDE DOWN ON THE 'WITCHES HAT' IN CLAYTON PARK
JUST FOR A LARK? – IT MADE YOU WONDER
WHAT THE SERVICES DID TO THESE POOR SOULS?

TAKING A STROLL DOWN NORTH ROAD, CLAYTON

PASSING THE INFAMOUS 'RED REC'
LETTING ON TO THE MAN WITH THE SWOLLEN HEAD
SITTING THERE LOOKING ALL FORLORN IN HIS WHEEL CHAIR
"WATER ON TH'BRAIN - POOR KID"
OUR MUM WOULD SAY "LIFE'S SO UNFAIR"

CALLING AT ALWYN GRIFFITHS FAMILY BUTCHER'S
AND ON TO NEXT DOOR'S GREEN GROCER'S
'GAMMY GITTEN' THE KIDS WOULD CRUELLY CALL
THE POOR 'OL HANDICAPPED SHOPKEEPER - MR. GITTEN

"WHAT DOO YOO WANNNT?" HE WOULD SAY
IN HIS 'PUNCH & JUDY' LIKE VOICE
THE KIDS WOULD MOCK AND MIMICK HIM

ANOTHER UNFORTUNATE KID CALLED EDDY
WHO WAS SO BADLY SCARRED, BRUISED & BATTERED
FROM ALL THOSE SEVERE AND HORRENDOUS EPILEPTIC FITS

HE SURVIVED EACH AND EVERY OTHER DAY
UNTIL HE HAD ONE TOO MANY - SWALLOWED HIS TONGUE
AND TRAGICALLY PASSED AWAY

ANOTHER SIMPLE SOUL WAS KEITH USUALLY PLACID,
HARMLESS AND SOFT
UNTIL HE WAS PROVOKED AND TAUNTED BY YOUNG MORONS
WHO THREW STONES AND CLUMPS OF GRASS SODS AT HIM
'TIL HE EVENTUALLY SNAPPED AND CHASED THEM
WILDLY OVER THE CROFT

ALFIE WAS THE NOTORIOUS 'BIKE THIEF'
A CHARACTER YOU DIDN'T WISH TO MEET
A DODGY, DEMONIC AND DECEITFUL DEVIL
WHO SPREAD INSTANT PANIC
WHEN HE WALKED SHAMELESSLY DOWN OUR STREET

THE RAG AND BONE MEN -
OWD 'SLAVER CHOPS' WHO SPLUTTERED & MUTTERED "'BONE! BONE!"

WHO ONCE GOT EXTREMELY UPSET -
WHEN SOME PRANKSTERS UP-ENDED HIS LADENED CART
THUS TIPPING HIS LOAD OF RAGS AND DONKEY STONES
ALL OVER THE ROAD AND GETTING THEM SOAKING WET

AND MR CRELLIN WHO LIKE THE ODD TIPPLE
AS US KIDS WOULD SING AND SHOUT
'LONE RANGER' STYLE - "HI! HO! CRELLIN AWAWWWWAYY!!!
AS HE STAGGERED AND SWAYED IN HIS USUAL DIRECTION
WITH HIS WOBBLIN' WHEELS AND RICKETY CART
TOWARDS THE 'CLAYTON VIC' FOR ANOTHER HEAVY SESSION.....

ON THE CORNER

WHERE US SPOTTY TEENAGERS WOULD MEET
IN OUR DEN - OUR LAIR
'DR. TAYLOR'S' SURGERY
CORNER OF NORTH ROAD,IN CLAYTON
COMPAIRING THE LENGTH OF OUR HAIR

I REMEMBER ONE OF THE LADS 'JIMMY PIFCO'
HAD HIS FLOWING LOCKS GROWN DOWN TO HIS BUM
IMPRESSING ALL THE GIRLS (ESPECIALLY HIS MUM!)

SITTING ON THE WALL, JUST LOAFIN' & LETCHIN'
AND TRYING DESPERATELY TO FLIRT
WITH THE LOCAL YOUNG SKIRT

PLAYING OUR EXTREMELY LOUD 'TRANNIES'-
TO OUR DESPAIRING MUMS & GRANNIES
LISTENING TO 'MY GENERATION' BY 'THE WHO'

"WHY DON'TCHA ALL F F F F FADE AWAY -
NOT TRY AN' DIG WHAT WE ALL SAY"

THIS WAS OUR WORLD THE SIXTIES
'TEENAGERS IN CREATION'

"NOT TRYIN' TO CAUSE A BIG SENSATION
 JUST TALKIN' 'BOUT MY G G GENERATION"

ON THE CORNER
EAGERLY ANTICIPATING THE FUTURE - OUR FUTURE
JUST WATCHIN' THE WORLD GOIN' BY

WITH AN AIR OF INNOCENCE
AND A GLEAM IN OUR EYE......

SHORT BACK & SIDES

I REMEMBER -
THE DAY MY DAD CHASED ME DOWN THE BACK
LIKE A PSYCHOPATH WIELDING AN AXE!
ONLY IT WAS WORSE - A PAIR OF SCISSORS
- TO HACK OFF MY REBELLIOUS, LONG, LANK HAIR
IT WAS AN ABSOLUTE NIGHTMARE!

HE UNFORTUNATELY CAUGHT ME
AND GAVE ME AN HORRENDOUS SHORT BACK & SIDES
I DIDN'T GO OUT FOR DAYS
AVOIDING ALL MY GIRLFRIENDS & MATES

I TRIED IN VAIN TO CONVINCE HIM
THAT IT WAS THE STYLE & FASHION
AND NOT BEING SO CALLED 'EFFEMINATE!'
BUT HE COULDN'T RELATE

"ROLLIN' RUDDY STONES -
BLOODY TARTS THESE DAYS" - HE'D GRUMBLE & SAY
THEN COMB HIS CURLY CROP & WALK DEJECTEDLY AWAY

FINALLY HE RELENTED
TO LET ME GROW MY HAIR LIKE I WANTED
- TO EMULATE MY HERO 'MICK JAGGER'

I'D JUMP UP, CLAP MY HANDS,
PUCKER UP & SWAGGER,
RUBBER-NECK, SHAKE MY HAIR,
RATTLE MY MARACAS & YELL -

"I'M A GONNA TELL YA
HOW IT'S GONNA BE
YOUR GONNA GIVE YOUR LOVE TO ME -

LOVE WILL LAST MORE THAN ONE DAY
COS LOVE IS LOVE
AND NOT FADE AWAY"......

FLITTING

MOVING FROM OUR RENTED CORPORATION TWO UP AND TWO DOWN
TERRACED HOUSE IN BARRINGTON STREET, CLAYTON IN 1963
TO A MORTGAGED BRAND SPANKING NEWLY BUILT THREE BED SEMI
WAS LIKE A DREAM COME TRUE

13 NORFOLK CRESCENT,
IN THE SUBURBAN AREA OF
FAILSWORTH, MANCHESTER
£2,000 IT COST MUM AND DAD
WHICH WAS A FORTUNE
IN THE EARLY SIXTIES
AND WITH FIVE KIDS - IT
WAS AN ABSOLUTE MIRACLE

DAD WAS A SKILLED
MAINTENANCE FOREMAN FITTER
AND WORKED FOR THE
'CLAYTON ANILINE COMPANY',

MUM WAS A HARDWORKING AND
EXTREMELY BUSY HOUSEWIFE
WHO WORKED PARTIME AT THE
LOCAL 'MALBOROUGH MILL',

US KIDS WILL ALWAYS BE
INDEBTED TO THEM
FOR HAVING THE COURAGE,
WILLINGNESS AND VISION
TO IMPROVE OUR FAMILY'S
QUALITY OF LIFE BY MAKING

THIS BRAVE DECISION
IT GAVE US ALL BETTER
OPPORTUNITIES

ESPECIALLY FOR
MY YOUNGER BRO'S
WHO GOT A BETTER EDUCATION
AND WENT ON TO ACHIEVE
UNIVERSITY DEGREES......

LAST TANGO IN FAILSWORTH

OUR MUM & DAD USED TO GO BALLROOM DANCING
AT THE 'COURT SCHOOL OF DANCING' IN STRETFORD
THEY CHA CHA CHA'D, TANGO'D, FOXTROTTED & CAUSED A COMMOTION
WHEN THEY DID THE MADISON, BOSSENOVA, TWIST & LOCOMOTION

THEY JITTERBUG'D - DID THE HUCKLEBUCK
TO THE 'STRAND SHOWBAND'
THEY MARCHED TO THE MARCH OF THE MODS

FOR THE ONE & ONLY 'JOE LOSS'
JIVING & JIGGING - SHUFFLING & SHIMMERING
THEY EVEN DID THE SLOSH

COLLECTING MEDALS BY THR SCORE
THEY WERE WIZARDS ON THAT DANCE FLOOR

DAD LIKED 'TOM JONES' WHICH WAS 'NOT UNUSUAL'
HE GREW SIDEBURNS AND WITH HIS CURLY HAIR
WAS A DEAD RINGER FOR HIM

MUM LIKED 'ELVIS' & 'P.J.PROBY'
ESPECIALLY WHEN HIS TROUSERS SPLIT ON STAGE
- THERE WAS AN OUTRAGE!

"HOLD ME, HONEY WON'T YOU HOLD ME"
& "THERE'S A PLACE FOR US SOMM-A-WHERE A PLACE FOR US"

THEY WALTZED WITH 'ENGLEBERT HUMPERDINCK'S' -
"I HAD THE LAST WALTZ WITH YOU"
& "PLEASE, RELEASE ME, LET ME GO"

MUM & DAD HAD LOTS OF PARTIES IN THEIR HEYDAY
AND THEY EVENTUALLY SUCCUMED TO 'THE BEATLES'
WHEN THEY SANG 'ALL MY LOVING' & 'YESTERDAY'

EVEN OUR GRAN LOVED 'ELVIS' AFTER THE INITIAL SHOCK & FRIGHT
OF SEEING HIM SHAKE HIS HIPS & BUM - ON THE TELLY ONE NIGHT

AND WHEN HE CAME OUT OF THE ARMY AND SANG
'IT'S NOW OR NEVER', 'WOODEN HEART',
'ARE YOU LONESOME TONIGHT' & 'SURRENDER'
SHE THOUGHT HE WAS VERY HANDSOME & A BIT OF ALRIGHT......

TOP TEN CLUB (BELLE VUE)

THE TOP TEN CLUB WAS HELD AT THE ELIZABETHAN HALL, I RECALL
WITH RESIDENT D.J.'S JIMMY SAVILLE ('HOWSABOUTTHATTHEN')
RAY TERET AND A LITTLE CURLY HAIRED GUY THEY CALLED TITCH
PLAYING ALL THE LATEST 45's IN THE N.M.E. TOP TEN

THEY HAD A REVOLVING STAGE
WHEN ONE LIVE GROUP FINISHED THEIR SET
ANOTHER ONE WOULD APPEAR AS IF BY MAGIC

I REMEMBER THE D.J. PLAYING 'GLAD ALL OVER'
BY THE DAVE CLARK FIVE
AND THE WHOLE DANCEFLOOR STOMPERS WOULD JUMP UP AND DOWN
TO THAT DRUM - THUMP! THUMP! SOUND

I ONCE WITNESSED 'THE PRETTY THINGS' ONE NIGHT
WHEN ALL THE GIRLS WENT FRANTIC AND IN A RAGE
AND TRIED TO PULL THE SINGER 'PHIL MAY' OFF THE STAGE

I ALSO EXPERIENCED THE MINDBLOWING MAGIC OF 'JIMI HENDRIX'
SETTING HIS GUITAR ALIGHT! ON STAGE - JUST FOR KIX

APPARENTLY ON ONE 'ROCKERAMA' NIGHT
WHEN ONE BUDDING NEW GROUP HAD FINISHED THEIR SET
THE OTHER UNFORTUNATE GROUP ROUND THE OTHER SIDE
HAD THEIR AMPS PLUGGED IN - AND READY TO ROCK

WHEN THE STAGE REVOLVED THEY HAD HELL OF A SHOCK
DUE TO HAVING 'SHORT LEADS'
THEY HAD THEIR AMPS DRAGGED OFF STAGE — WHAT AN OUTRAGE!

TRYING TO COP OFF IN SUCH A MASSIVE CLUB WAS A CRIME
DUE TO THEIR BEING SO MANY MINI-SKIRTED GORGEOUS GIRLS

WHICH CONFUSED AND BEMUSED OUR POOR PEVERTED TEENAGE MINDS
SO INVARIABLY WE ALWAYS SCORED IN INJURY TIME......

BEAT CITY (EX-THREE COINS)

THE BEAT CITY WAS IN FOUNTAIN STREET NEAR THE TOWN HALL
OWNED BY BIG 'BARRY COLLENS' A MAN ABOUT TOWN
WHO WAS REPUTED TO BE A BIT OF A PERV.
ACCORDING TO THE GIRLS WHO FLIRTED AROUND

I REMEMBER ONE ANKLE LENGTH HAIRY, ACNE FACED
GROUP CALLED 'THE MYAX'
WHO WERE ALWAYS AS HIGH AS MR. KITE
PLAYING RAUNCHY BLUES ALMOST EVERY NIGHT

"I'M HER YESTERDAY MAN" - SANG A SAD CHRIS ANDREWS
- "WELL MY FRIENDS THAT'S WHAT I AM"

AS WE ALL SANG ALONG TO "HERE COMES THE NIGHT"
AND "GLORIA - G-L-O-R-I-A, GLORIA" BY VAN MORRISON'S THEM

"I'M IN WITH THE IN CROWD, I GO WHERE THE IN CROWD GO"
AND "AT THE DISCO - TAY! - HEY! HEY! HEY!"
SANG SOUL SINGER DOBIE GRAY

"DO YOU BELIEVE IN MAGIC" SANG THE LOVING SPOONFUL
"ONE TWO THREE - THAT'S HOW ELEMENTARY IT'S GONNA BE -
LIKE TAKING CANDY FROM A BABY"
AS WE DANCED SEDUCTIVELY TO LEN BARRY

THIS WAS ONE OF THE BEST CLUBS AROUND TOWN - BEAT CITY
WHERE THE GUYS WERE COOL AND GIRLS SO SEXY AND PRETTY

EVEN 'JIMMY SAVILLE' WAS OFTEN SEEN FLITTING AROUND
HE WAS SUCH AN APPROACHABLE CHARACTER
WHO HAD TIME FOR EVERYONE - HE WAS SOUND......

THE THREE COINS

'THE BEATLES' HAD PLAYED AT 'THE THREE COINS' IN 1962
ONE NIGHT FOR £5.00 THEY CREATED SUCH A BUZZ
THEY ACTUALLY GOT A RISE THE SECOND NIGHT £25.00
THIS IS ABSOLUTELY TRUE - JIMMY SAVILLE TOLD US!

TOP TWENTY CLUB (DROYLSDEN)

WAS ALSO OWNED BY BIG BARRY COLLENS
RESIDENT D.J.'S WERE DAVE EAGER, DAVE BOOTH AND BILLY Q.T.
(WHO INCIDENTLY WAS A BIT OF A CUTIE!)

I RECALL SOME OF THE ACTS THAT APPEARED ON THE T.T.
LIKE DAVE DEE, DOZEY, BEAKY, MICK AND TITCH -
"HOLD TIGHT COUNT TO THREE, GOTTA STAY CLOSE TO ME"
AND "'BEND IT! BEND IT! JUST A LITTLE BIT"
WELL - BILLY Q.T.'S EYES LIT UP WHEN THEY SANG THIS HIT

LOS BRAVOS WHO SANG - "BLACK IS BLACK, I WANT MY BABY BACK"
REVERAND BLACK AND THE ROCKIN' VICARS -
"SKINNY MINNY, SHE AIN'T SKINNY, SHE'S TALL, THAT'S ALL"

LOCAL ACTS LIKE THE FACTOTEMS
DROYLSDENS ANSWER TO THE BEACH BOYS WERE ON ALL THE TIME
WE USED TO HAVE A GIGGLE AT THE SINGER
COS' HE COULN'T SING AND PLAY HIS GUITAR AT THE SAME TIME

FRANKENSTEIN AND THE MONSTERS WERE A SUPERB ACT
REALLY SHIT SCAREY! - IT WAS ABSOLUTE CARNAGE
WHEN HE JUMPED, TERRIFYINGLY OFF THE STAGE
CHASING THE GIRLS WHO WOULD SCREAM HYSTERICALLY
SCATTER AND GRAB HOLD OF THE BIGGEST AND BRAVEST LADS
THEY COULD FIND OR FANCIED REALLY!

 MIND YOU - QUITE A FEW OF THE LADS LEGGED IT
COS' FRANKY WAS AWESOME AND ABOUT SEVEN FOOT TWO

I REMEMBER BREAKING MY WRIST PLAYING FOOTY
DOING A DENIS LAW OVERHEAD KICK
MISSING THE BALL BY A MILE
& LANDING HEAVY ON MY WRIST - WHAT A DICK!

GOING TO THE T.T. CLUB WITH MY PLASTERCAST ON
SEEMED TO ATTRACT THE GIRLS WHO TOOK PITY ON ME
WHICH I TOOK MAXIMUM ADVANTAGE OF - YOU SEE
ESPECIALLY WITH SEXY JANICE WHO STOLE THE VIRGINITY
OF THIS POOR OL' ONE ARM LAD - WHOPPEEE!!

ON FRIDAY'S AT THE END OF THE NIGHT, I WOULD SPRINT ALL THE
WAY BACK HOME TO FAILSWORTH - ABOUT FIVE MILES OR MORE

POUNDING & POUNDING, HUFFIN' & PUFFIN', GIVING IT SOME WELLY
SO I COULD WATCH 'READY STEADY GO' WITH 'KEITH FORDYCE'
AND THE FAB & GORGEOUS 'CATHY MCGOWAN' ON THE TELLY......

JUNGFRAU

IN CATHEDRAL STREET OPPOSITE 'MANCHESTER CATHEDRAL'
WAS A GREAT LITTLE CLUB THAT HAD TOP GROUPS ON
IT ALSO HAD MIMING CONTESTS INBETWEEN THE ACTS
MIMING TO 'MICK JAGGER' WAS EVERYBODIES FAVOURITE ONE

WITH HIS CHICKEN RUBBER NECKIN' STRUTT & POUTING LIPS
MY MATE 'NOBBY' WOULD SWIVEL HIS HIPS
AND WHEN HE WAGGLED HIS BUM -
THEIR WAS NO CONTEST - HE ALWAYS WON

WHEN 'GEORGIE BEST' APPEARED LOOKIN' TRENDY & COOL
ALL THE GIRLS WOULD TURN AND DROOL
THUS IGNORING US 'HORNY HERBERTS'
WHO'D BUGGER OFF TO 'THE MITRE' ACROSS THE WAY
FOR A COUPLE OF PINTS - LOOKIN' FOR A GOOD LAY……

LE PHONAGRAPHE

WAS AN EXCLUSIVE CLUB FOR T.V. CELEBS
TRENDY POP & FOOTBALL STARS -
LIKE 'THE HOLLIES', 'HERMANS HERMITS'
'GEORGE BEST' & 'RODNEY MARSH'
WITH THEIR TRENDY CLOTHES & POSH CARS

ME & MY MATE DENIS CONNED OUR WAY IN ONE NIGHT
GOT DRINKS & NECKED THEM BY THE SCORE
(THEY KEPT A CHITTY AT THE BAR)

THEN WHEN WE SAW THE ASTRONOMICAL BILL
BEING EVER SO DISCREET -
DID A RUNNER DOWN JOHN DALTON STREET……

1965

WAS THE YEAR OL' WARHORSE 'WINSTON CHURCHILL' PASSED AWAY
AT 91 YEARS OF AGE - A STATE FUNERAL WAS ARRANGED
IT WAS ALSO THE YEAR THAT OUR DEAR GRANDMA PASSED AWAY
AN EXTREMELY SAD DAY FOR OUR FAMILY

'THE BEATLES' WERE AWARDED M.B.E.'S
BY HER MAJESTY THE QUEEN
MANCHESTER GROUPS 'WAYNE FONTANA & THE MINDBENDERS',
'HERMAN'S HERMITS' & 'FREDDY & THE DREAMERS'
SCORED THE U.S.A. CHARTS WITH A HAT TRICK No.1, No.2 & No.3
A FANTASTIC FEAT FOR OUR PROUD CITY

AND 'THE HOLLIES' HAD THEIR FIRST
U.K. No.1 HIT WITH 'I'M ALIVE', GEORDIES OWN 'THE ANIMALS'
HAD CHARTED WITH 'BRING IT ON HOME',
'WE'VE GOTTA GET OUT OF THIS PLACE', & 'IT'S MY LIFE',

YOUNG COCKNEY MODS 'THE SMALL FACES'
HAD THEIR FIRST HIT WITH 'WATCHA GONNA DO 'BOUT IT,
& THE 'KINKS' HAD A No.1 WITH 'TIRED OF WAITING FOR YOU'
MEANWHILE 'THE WALKER BRO'S' HAD INVADED THE BRITISH SHORES
WITH 'LOVE HER', 'MAKE IT EASY ON YOURSELF'
& 'MY SHIP IS COMING IN'

'BOB DYLAN' HAD INVADED THE SHORES TOO
WITH THREE L.P.'S IN THE CHARTS 'TIMES THEY ARE A-CHANGIN',
'ANOTHER SIDE OF BOB DYLAN' & 'THE FREEWHEELIN' BOB DYLAN'
'THE BYRDS' HAD A HIT WITH BOB DYLAN'S 'MR. TAMBOURINE MAN'
ALONG WITH 'CHER'S' - 'ALL I REALLY WANNA DO'
& 'JOAN BAEZ' ENTERED THE TOP TEN
WITH CIVIL RIGHTS SONG 'WE SHALL OVERCOME'

ANOTHER PROTEST SINGER FROM CANADA WAS CAMPAIGNER FOR
INDIAN RIGHTS - 'BUFFY SAINT-MARIE' WHO SANG THE THEME SONG
FOR THE CONTROVERSIAL MOVIE 'SOLDIER BLUE'
GLASGOW BORN 'DONOVAN' WAS OUR ANSWER TO 'BOB DYLAN'
A STREET BUSKER WHO APPEARED ON 'READY STEADY GO'
HE ALSO HAD SUCCESS WITH 'CATCH THE WIND' & 'COLOURS'

'THE STONES' HAD TWO ABSOLUTE CLASSICS IN 65 -
'SATISFACTION' & 'GET OFF MY CLOUD'
EVEN COMEDIAN 'KEN DODD' HAD A No.1 WITH 'TEARS FOR
SOUVENIRS' TO END ANOTHER MUSICALLY CHALLENGED YEAR......

T.V. (SIXTIES)

'FOUR FEATHER FALLS'-
WITH TEX TUCKER, BIG BAD BEN & PEDRO THE BANDIT,
'FIREBALL XL5' WITH COL. STEVE ZODIAC & ROBERT THE ROBOT

'STINGRAY' WITH TROY TEMPEST & MERMAID AQUA MARINA
'SUPERCAR' WITH MIKE MERCURY & MITCH THE MONKEY
'JOE 90' & 'THUNDERBIRDS' WITH LADY PENELOPE
AND PARKER - "YUS MULADY!"

"TORCHY, TORCHY THE BATTERY BOY - HE'S A WALKY TALKY TOY"
'CAMBERWICK GREEN' AND 'TRUMPTON'S FAMOUS FIRE BRIGADE -
"HUGH, PUGH, BARNEY McGREW, CUTHBERT, DIGGLE AND GRUB"

'THE HUCKLEBERRY HOUND SHOW' WITH 'YOGI BEAR AND BOO BOO'
'THE FLINTSTONES' FREDDIE FLINTSTONE "YABBA! DABBA! DOO!"
AND HIS HAPLESS SIDEKICK BARNEY RUBBLE
ALWAYS UP TO MISCHIEF AND TROUBLE

'THE JETSONS' FUTURISTIC FAMILY
'SKIPPY THE BUSH KANGEROO'
'FLIPPER' THE FRIENDLY DOLPHIN

'DAKTARI' WITH CLARENCE THE CROSS-EYED LION
REMEMBER 'SNAGGLEPUSS' - "HEAVENS TO MURGATROYD"
"EXIT STAGE LEFT - EVEN" - THE CUNNING OL' LION
'THE CLANGERS' WITH THE FROGLETS AND THE SOUP DRAGON

'HECTORS HOUSE' AND 'THE MAGIC ROUNDABOUT' -
WITH DOPEY DYLAN - "HEY MANNN!", DOUGALL, ERMINTRUDE
AND ZEBEDEE - BOING! BOING!
'WALLY WHYTON AND OLLIE BEAK', 'BASIL BRUSH' BUM! BUM!

CRUSTY OL' SEA DOG 'CAPTAIN PUGWASH' -
"HEY! HO! MI HEARTIES!" WITH THE CREW OF THE BLACK PIG -
ROGER THE CABIN BOY, SEAMAN STAINS AND MASTER BATES
(DID ANYBODY TAKE NOTE?) VERSUS THE EVIL CUT-THROAT JAKE

'THE WACKY RACES' WITH DIRTY DICK DASTARDLY
AND MUTTLEY HIS ASMATIC LAUGHING DOG,
'PENELOPE PITSTOP' AND 'THE ANTHILL MOB'
'DOCTOR WHO' AND THE DALEKS - "EXTERMINATE! EXTERMINATE!"
'GILLIGANS ISLE' AND 'MY FAVOURITE MARTIAN' WERE GREAT

'THE BEVERLEY HILLBILLIES' WITH BIG AND DAFT JETHRO,
ELLE MAY AND GRANNY WITH HER POSSUM BELLY STEW

THE EDUCATIONAL 'MAGPIE' AND 'BLUE PETER' TO NAME TWO
WITH VAL SINGLETON, PETER PURVES, JOHN NOAKES AND SHEP
'RAINBOW' WITH BUNGLE AND ZIPPY - "JEFFREEE!!"

'CRACKERJACK' WITH AEMON ANDREWS -
"DOUBLE OR DROP?" - STICK ANOTHER CABBAGE ON TOP!
POOR OL'LOSER GOT HIS CRACKERJACK PENCIL - WHAT A SOP!

THE FIRST EPISODES OF 'CORONATION STREET'
WITH ELSIE TANNER, ENA SHARPLES, MINNIE CALDWELL
HER CAT BOBBY, MARTHA LONGHURST, FLORRIE LINDLEY
THE HEWITTS, THE BARLOWS, THE OGDENS & LEONARD SWINDLEY

'JUKEBOX JURY' WITH DAVID JACOBS
'THANK YOUR LUCKY STARS' WITH BRIAN MATTHEW
WITH BRUMMIE JANICE - "I'LL GIVE IT FOIVE!"

'TOP OF THE POPS' WITH SEXY PANS PEOPLE - HAVIN' A JIVE
'READY STEADY GO' WITH KEITH FORDYCE AND CATHY McGOWAN

'OPPORTUNITY KNOCKS' WITH KING OF CORN MR.HUGHIE GREEN
"YOU WANNA HEAR IT FOLKS?" - A CRINGE FOR US BLOKES

"77 SUNSET STRIP - CLICK! CLICK!"
STARRING EFREM ZIMBALIST JUNIOR & HIS SIDE KICK -
THE QUIFF COMBING ED BURNES AS 'COOKIE'

ACE CRIMINAL LAWYER - RAYMOND BURR IN 'PERRY MASON'

'THE NAKED CITY' -
"THERE ARE EIGHT MILLION STORIES IN THE NAKED CITY
- THIS HAS BEEN ONE OF THEM"

'THE ADVENGERS' - THE ELEGANT PATRICK McNEE AS JOHN STEED
SEXY HONOUR BLACKMAN AS CATHY GALE
DRESSED IN BLACK LEATHER - PWOORR!!

ALSO DIANA RIGG AS EMMA PEEL
LINDA THORSON AS TARA KING -
ALL SEXSATIONAL AND UNREAL

WHILE MUM AND OUR GRAN OGLED - 'DR. FINLEY'S CASEBOOK'
AND 'THE FORSYTHE SAGA' - (WITH SEXY NYREE DAWN PORTER)

KNITTING BY THE FIRESIDE AND DROOLIN' OVER GRAN'S IDOL
JACK WARNER "EVENING ALL" IN 'DIXON OF DOCK GREEN'

US KIDS WERE GLUED TO THE SCREEN –
TO VIEW 'THE SAINT' WITH SUAVE ROGER MOORE

'DANGERMAN' AND 'THE PRISONER' WITH PATRICK McGOOHAN
'I SPY' AND 'SPECIAL BRANCH'

'THE MAN FROM UNCLE' AGAINST ARCH ENEMIES 'THRUSH'
WITH SPECIAL AGENTS ROBERT VAUGHAN AS NAPOLEAN SOLO
AND DAVID McCALLUM AS ILYA KURYAKIN

'CALLAN' WAS EDWARD WOODWARD WITH RUSSEL HUNTER AS LONELY
MAGILL PLAYED BY RICHARD BRADFORD IN 'MAN IN A SUITCASE'

'MISSION IMPOSSIBLE' AND 'LOST IN SPACE'
'VOYAGE TO THE BOTTOM OF THE SEA'
WHICH HAD YOU FELLING SEA-SICK AS THE BOAT WENT
ROCKIN' FROM ONE SIDE TO THE NEXT INCESSANTLY

'THE TIME TUNNEL' AND 'THE LAND OF GIANTS'
'THE MUNSTERS' AND 'THE ADAMS FAMILY'

'HAWII FIVE-O' AND 'THE INVISIBLE MAN' –
(COULDN'T THINK WHAT THEY SAW IN HIM?)

'THE FUGITIVE' WAS RICHARD KIMBLE PLAYED BY DAVID JANSEN
DID THEY EVER CATCH THE ONE ARM MAN?

'THE INVADERS'– WITH THOSE STIFF LITTLE FINGERS –
DID THIS EVER END?

'DEPARTMENT S' WITH SUAVE JASON KING
'STARTREK' WITH CAPTAIN KIRK – "BEAM ME UP SCOTTIE!"
AND THE UNEMOTIONAL ALIEN – MR.SPOCK

'DADS ARMY' WITH POMPOUS ATHUR LOWE
AS CAPTAIN MANWAIRING – "STUPID BOY! PIKE"

'THE LIVERBIRDS' POLLY JAMES AS DOTTY BERYL
AND NERYS HUGHES AS THE SOPHISICATED SANDRA

'THE LIKELY LADS' WITH BOB AND TERRY
– "BY THE CRINGE"
ALIAS JAMES BOLAN AND RODNEY BEWES

'SCENE AT SIX THIRTY' FOLLOWED
BY 'Z CARS' & 'CROSSROADS'

'ARMCHAIR THEATRE',
ROAL DAHL'S 'TALES OF THE UNEXPECTED'
HAD US SHAKIN' IN OUR SHOES

'THE UNTOUCHABLES' WITH ROBERT STACK AS ELLIOT NESS
CHASING MOBSTERS AL CAPONE, BUGS MORAN AND THE REST

'STEPTOE & SON' WITH HARRY H CORBERT & WILFRED BRAMBLE
"YOU THE DIRTY OL' MAN"

'TIL DEATH US DO PART' WITH BIGOTTED ALF GARNETT
ALIAS WARREN MITCHELL WOULD CAUSE AN UPSET

WITH ANTHONY BOOTH "THE RANDY SCOUSE GIT"
MARRIED TO DAUGHTER RITA - UNA STUBBS
AND "SILLY OL' MOO" MUM ELSE - DANDY NICHOLS

COWY'S -
'THE LONE RANGER' - "HI HO SILVER AWAAAAY"
WITH HIS INDIAN SCOUT 'TONTO'

'CHEYENNE' BODIE (LONELY MAN),

'GUNSMOKE', 'THE MAN FROM LARAMIE',
'HAVE GUN, WILL TRAVEL'
AND 'WELLS FARGO'

'THE HIGH CHAPARRAL' -
WITH BIG JOHN CANNON, SON BLUE,
DAUGHTER VICTORIA
& BRO' IN-LAW MANOLITO

'BONANZA' WITH THE CARTWRIGHTS
BEN, HOSS & LITTLE JOE

'THE BIG VALLEY', 'THE VIRGINIAN'
AND 'BRANDED' -
WITH BIG CHUCK CONNORS AS JASON McCORD

ALSO UGLY MUG REECE -
"AW I AIN'T THAT BAD" IN 'LAREDO'

'RAWHIDE' WITH CLINT EASTWOOD AS ROWDY YATES
'WAGON TRAIN' WITH ROBERT HORTON AS FLINT McCULLOUGH

THOSE SATIRE SHOWS LIKE –
'BEYOND THE FRINGE'
AND 'THAT WAS THE WEEK THAT WAS'

WITH DAVID FROST, ROY KINNEAR,
LANCE PERCIVAL, WILLIAM RUSHTON,
JOHN BIRD, JOHN WELLS, RONNIE BARKER,

RONNIE CORBET,
ELEANOR BRON AND MILLICENT MARTIN

PETE & DUD IN 'NOT ONLY BUT ALSO'
THAT WE 'FOUGHT WAS FANNEE!'
THOUGH IT NEVER AMUSED OUR GRANNY

NEITHER DID 'ROWAN AND MARTIN'S LAUGH IN'
WITH DIZZY BLOND THE HORNY GOLDIE HAWN
– YOU DIDN'T KNOW YOU WERE BORN!

THEN CAME 'MONTY PYTHON'S FLYING CIRCUS'
SURREAL COMEDY FROM – JOHN CLEESE,
MICHAEL PALIN, ERIC IDOL,
GRAHAM CHAPMAN,
TERRY JONES AND TERRY GILLIAM
ABSOLUTE GENIUS'S – BRILLIANT

THOSE VARIETY SHOWS -

'THE BLACK & WHITE MINSTREL SHOW'
WITH THE DENNIS MITCHELL SINGERS
(WHICH WAS LATER BANNED FOR BEING RACIST)

'SATURDAY NIGHT AT THE LONDON PALLADIUM'
WITH BRUCE FORSYTH - "I'M IN CHARGE!"
LATER NORMAN VAUGHAN -"SWINGIN! OOH! DODGY!"
REMEMBER THAT NERVE WRACKIN' BEAT THE CLOCK

ALONG WITH THE ROYAL COMMAND PERFORMANCES
THAT FEATURD TOP COMEDIANS LIKE -

DAVE ALLEN, JIMMY TARBUK, TOMMY COOPER "JUST LIKE THAT!"
DRUNKS - THE FABULOUS FREDDY FRINTON & JIMMY JEWEL

MORCAMBE AND WISE (WITH HIS SHORT FAT HAIRY LEGS)
FRANKY HOWARD "OOOOH! PEOPLE! I SAY!"

NORMAN WISDOM "DON'T LAUGH AT ME COS I'M A FOOL"
"HELLO MY DARLIN'S" - CHARLIE DRAKE
MADE YOU LAUGH 'TIL YOUR SIDES ACHED

TOP GROUPS LIKE THE BEATLES -
REMEMBER JOHN LENNON'S BIT OF TOM FOOLERY -
"THOSE OF YOU SAT IN THE CHEAP SEATS CLAP YOUR HANDS,
THE REST RATTLE YOUR JEWELLRY"

AND THE REBELLIOUS ROLLING STONES
WHO REFUSED TO RIDE ON
THAT ROUNDABOUT AND WAVE
AT THE END OF THE SHOW -
I MEAN IT WOULD HAVE SPOILED THEIR WILD ROCKERS IMAGE
- QUITE RIGHT TOO!......

THE MUSICALS

'HELLO DOLLY', THE SONG TITLE WAS A MASSIVE HIT FOR
OL' GRAVEL VOICE 'SATCHMO' - LOUIS ARMSTRONG

TOMMY STEELE'S PRODUCTION OF 'HALF A SIXPENCE'
WITH THAT CORNY 'FLASH! BANG! WALLOP!' SONG

LIONEL BART'S 'OLIVER'-
WITH "CONSIDER YOURSELVES ONE OF US
CONSIDER YOURSELVES ONE OF THE FAMILY"
SUNG BY THE ARTFUL DODGER AND CO.

MEL BROOKES'S CONTROVERSIAL 'THE PRODUCERS'

HAIR' - THE HIPPY MUSICAL THAT WAS ALMOST OBSCENE
WITH IT'S SHOCKING FULL FRONTAL NUDE SCENES

AND GREAT SONGS LIKE -
'THE DAWNING OF THE AGE OF AQUARIUS',

'HARE KRISHNA', 'GOOD MORNING STARSHINE'
'LET THE SUNSHINE IN' SUNG BY 'THE TRIBE'

AND 'AIN'T GOT NO - I GOT LIFE'
WHICH WAS A MASSIVE HIT FOR NINA SIMONE......

FASHIONS & STYLES

REMEMBER THOSE DRIP-DRY
BRY-NYLON COOL CREAM
& SNOW WHITE SHINEY SHIRTS
EASY TO WASH, DIDN'T SHRINK,
INSTANT DRYING, NO IRONING
WAS AN ABSOLUTE BLESSING FOR OUR MUMS -
DON'T YA THINK!

ALTHOUGH THE NOVELTY SOON WORE OFF
DUE TO OUR EXTREMELY
SWEATY TEENAGE ARMPITS
COS THEY WOULN'T LET YOUR BODY BREATHE
AND WENT A FUNNY SHADE OF YELLOW
THAT MADE US GUYS PEN AND INK!

OUR AUNTIE ALWYN & UNCLE DON
HAD EMIGRATED TO CANADA
THEN MOVED TO CONNECTICUT,
NEW ENGLAND, U.S.A
THEY WOULD SENT ME & MY
BROTHERS TRENDY FASHIONABLE
CLOTHES
FROM THE STATES TO DISPLAY

FROM THOSE MOP TOP
BEATLE HAIR CROPS,
TO THE ROLLING STONES, SHAGGY,
LANK & LONG HAIRED DOWN YER
BACK LOOKS

THE NEW STYLES WERE IN -
CHECK HIPSTER'S
THAT SHOWED YOUR 'BUILDERS BUM'

EVERY TIME YOU BENT DOWN
WHEN YOU DROPPED A HALF-A-CROWN
THEY WERE SO TIGHT
THEY BROUGHT TEARS TO YOUR EYES

BLACK POLO-NECK SWEATERS &
DR.KILDARE SHIRTS,
A 'JOHN LENNON' LEATHER CAP,
BLACK LEATHER JERKIN
WITH MATCHING LEATHER PANTS YOU
LOOKED A TREAT!
PURCHASED USUALLY FROM 'THE
TOGGERY' IN STOCKPORT,
'JONATHON SILVER'S' OFF
ST.ANNES SQUARE OR 'JEFFREY'S

BOUTIQUE' IN BROWN STREET, JUST OFF MARKET STREET

BELL BOTTOM FRAYED & TASSLED BLEACHED JEANS
CUBAN HEELS & CHELSEA BOOTS
MOCCASINS, JESUS BOOTS (SANDALS)
KAFTANS' HIPPY BEADS, ELEPHANT CORDS & CRUSHED VELVET FLARES

MOVING FROM THOSE MARY QUANT MICRO MINI SKIRTS
MODELLED 'SEX'SATIONALLY BY 'TWIGGY' AND 'THE SHRIMP'
(GIRL IN A MINI GETTING OUT OF A MINI)
THAT TURNED US HORNY TEENIES INTO DERANGED PERVES

TO BORING MAXI'S AND CHEESECLOTH DRESSES
WORN BY THOSE LIBERATING LASSES

DISSING THOSE 'HANK JANSEN' NOVELS
HENRY MILLER'S 'THE CARPETBAGGERS' & MUCKY PARADE MAGS

WE WERE NOW IDENTIFYING WITH AND GETTING OFF TO
THE PROTEST SONGS & LYRICS OF JOAN BAEZ AND BOB DYLAN

THE POT SMOKIN' POETRY OF ALAN GINSBERG & FERLINGHETTI
THE DEEP, MANIC AND SERIOUS STUFF OF LEONARD COHEN

THE LIVERPOOL BEAT POETS - ADRIAN MITCHELL,
ADRIAN HENRY, BRIAN PATTEN & ROGER McGOUGH

SOAKIN' IN HEAVY RUSSIAN LITERATURE
LIKE 'WAR & PEACE' BY TOLSTOY

'CRIME & PUNISHMENT' BY DOSTOEVSKY
'ONE DAY IN THE LIFE OF IVAN DENOSOVITCH' BY SOLZHENITSYN
THIS IS WHERE WE WERE GOING -

SAT CONTENT, JUST READING LOTS OF PHILOSOPHICAL BOOKS
IN AN OILSKIN MAC, A PAIR OF OL' FRAYED LEVIS

GRANDAD'S OLD CRAVAT, A COMBAT JACKET (WITH BULLET HOLES IN)
ADORNED WITH C.N.D. BADGES, A 'HALF A DOLLAR' WAISTCOAT FROM
THE LOCAL ARMY & NAVY STORES
ROLLING A SPLIFF, JUST TAKING IT ALL IN

AND OF COURSE NOT FORGETTING THOSE 'MODS' V. 'ROCKER WARS -
MODS IN BRACES, WEARING FINE SUITS OF MOHAIR, PORK PIE HATS,
PARKERS (OVERWHELMED WITH BADGES)
RIDING SCOOTERS - VESPAS & LAMBRETTAS
WITH LOTS OF LITTLE MIRRORS EVERWHERE

AND 'ROCKERS' (GREASERS) ON 500cc NORTONS
CLAD IN STUDDED BLACK LEATHER TASSLED JACKETS
WEARING SKIN TIGHT ICE BLUE JEANS AND THOSE
(KICK YER BLEEDIN' 'ED IN) JACK BOOTS

MOD'S VERSUS ROCKERS –
INTENSE WAS THE HATE
THERE WERE BATTLES &
SCUFFLES EVERYWHERE

ESPECIALLY AT
SOUTHERN SEA-SIDE
RESORTS LIKE BRIGHTON,
CLACTON-ON-SEA
AND MARGATE......

MY BRO. PHIL (THE MOD)

MOVIES (THE SIXTIES)

'G.I. BLUES' & 'BLUE HAWII' WERE ELVIS'S BEST FILMS TO DATE
CLIFF'S - 'THE YOUNG ONES' & 'SUMMER HOLIDAY' WERE O.K.ISH
BUT THE BEATLES -'A HARD DAY'S NIGHT' & 'HELP' - WERE GREAT

JAMES BOND FILMS - 'DR.NO', 'FROM RUSSIA WITH LOVE',
'GOLDFINGER', 'YOU ONLY LIVE TWICE' & 'THUNDERBALL'
STARRED SEAN CONNERY WHO PLAYED AGENT 007 IN THEM ALL

CULT FILMS (STARRING WORKING CLASS ACTORS)
 LIKE - 'THE L-SHAPED ROOM', 'A KIND OF LOVING',
'ROOM AT THE TOP' - WITH LAURENCE HARVEY AS JOE LAMPTON
'THE KNACK' WITH RITA TUSHINGHAM & 'A TASTE OF HONEY'

'ALFIE' WAS COCKNEY MICHAEL CANE WITH CO-STAR JANE ASHER
'BILLY LIAR' WAS TOM COURTNEY
'CHARLEY BUBBLES', 'SATURDAY NIGHT & SUNDAY MORNING' -
"DON'T LET THE BASTARDS GRIND YER DOWN"
STATED -'ARTHUR SEATON' ALIAS ALBERT FINNEY

'BLOW-UP' STARRED VANESSA REDGRAVE & DAVID HEMMINGS
WITH IT'S STRANGE, WEIRD AND SURREAL ENDING
'BARBARELLA' WAS SEXY JANE FONDA -
A FUTURISTIC SPACE ADVENTURE - UNFURLED
PLANET OF THE APES' WITH CHARLTON HESTON & RODDY McDOWALL
'2001 A SPACE ODYSSEY' WERE OUT OF THIS WORLD

THOSE SPAGHETTI WESTERNS -
'A FISTFUL OF DOLLARS',
'FOR A FEW DOLLARS MORE' AND
'THE GOOD, THE BAD & THE UGLY'

WITH THE COOL -
CLINT EASTWOOD & LEE VON CLEEF
THOSE PAIR OF GUNSLINGING CAHOOT'S -
SQUINTING THEIR EYES
AND SMOKIN' CHEROOT'S
PSYCHIN' EACH OTHER OUT
BEFORE THOSE GUNSMOKIN' SHOOT OUTS

'CAT BALLOU' WITH LEE MARVIN
AND JANE FONDA
'LITTLE BIG MAN' WAS DUSTIN HOFFMAN
'A MAN CALLED HORSE' WITH RICHARD HARRIS

'MIDNIGHT COWBOY' WITH JOHN VOIGHT AND DUSTIN HOFFMAN
'PAINT YOUR WAGON' WITH GRUFF COWBOY LEE MARVIN
SINGING "I WAS BORN UNDER A WANDERING STAR"

'COOL HAND LUKE' WAS COOL PAUL NEWMAN IN HIS PRIME
AS A TOUGH COWBOY IN 'BUTCH CASSIDY & THE SUNDANCE KID'
WITH SIDEKICK ROBERT REDFORD AS CO-PARTNER'S IN CRIME

'BONNIE & CLYDE' WITH WARREN BEATTY AND FAYE DUNAWAY
AS BLOODLUSTING BANK ROBBERS OF THEIR DAY

TO 'SOLDIER BLUE' - WITH ITS CONTROVERSIAL REALISM
(SHOWING THE INDIANS SIDE OF THE STORY)
HIGHLIGHTING THE BLOODY BATTLE SCENES

THAT WERE GRUESOME, BRUTAL AND GORY
AS THE CAVALRY ATTACKED PEACEFUL INDIAN SETTLEMENTS
KILLING MEN, RAPING WOMEN & CHILDREN FOR POWER AND GLORY

AND BACK TO FANTASY WITH 'THE MAGNIFICENT 7'
WITH STEVE McQUEEN, JAMES COCKBURN,
CHARLES BRONSON & TELLY SAVALAS -
WHO ALL STARRED IN 'THE RETURN OF THE SEVEN'

CULTURE CLASSICS LIKE - THOMAS HARDY'S
'FAR FROM THE MADDING CROWD'
STARRED TERENCE STAMP, ALAN BATES,
PETER FINCH & JULIE CHRISTY

'WOMEN IN LOVE' WITH ALAN BATES AND RUGGED OLIVER REED -
DOING THAT NUDE WRESTLING SCENE WHICH ALSO STARRED -
GLENDA JACKSON AND STEPHANIE BEACHAM - WHAT A TEAM!

MAGGIE SMITH WAS IN HER ACTING 'PRIME OF MISS JEAN BRODIE'
'IN THE HEAT OF THE NIGHT' WITH ROD STEIGER & SIDNEY POITIER

"BORN TO BE WI-I-I-I-I-ILLLD" - 'EASY RIDER'
WITH BIKER'S PETER FONDA AND DENNIS HOPPER
'GIRL ON A MOTORCYCLE' WITH THE FATEFULL
MARRIANE FAITHFULL - COMING A CROPPER!

'THE CHARGE OF THE LIGHT BRIGADE' WITH DAVID HEMMINGS
'LAWRENCE OF ARABIA' WITH PETER O'TOOLE AND OMAR SHERIF

'SPARTACUS' WITH OLD BUM CHIN KIRK DOUGLAS AND TONY CURTIS

'HERCULES UNCHAINED' & OTHER GREEK MYTHOLOGY FILMS
 WITH MUSCLE MEN STEVE REEVES AND VICTOR MATURE

'ZORBA THE GREEK' WAS ANTHONY QUINN

'DOCTOR ZIVARGO' WITH JULIE CHRISTY AND OMAR SHERIF
'ZULU' WITH MICHAEL CANE - WERE TERRIFIC

AS WAS 'THE GREATEST STORY EVER TOLD' -A BIBLICAL EPIC
'KRAKATOA - EAST OF JAVA' - ALL THAT LAVA!

AND THE BIG SCREEN MUSICALS THAT WERE TERRIFIC -
LIKE 'THE SOUND OF MUSIC'
WITH JULIE ANDREWS & CHRISTOPHER PLUMBER

'HELLO! DOLLY', 'OLIVER', 'MY FAIR LADY'
AND 'THOROUGHLY MODERN MILLIE'
AND THE LONGEST RUNNING MUSICAL 'SOUTH PACIFIC'

CRAZY CARRY ON FILMS WITH SYD JAMES, HATTY JAQUES,
BARBARA WINDSOR, CHARLES HAWTREY,
PETER BUTTERWORTH, KENNETH WILLIAMS,
SILVIA SIMMS, KENETH CONNOR,
JIM DALE AND BERNARD BRESSLAW

THE PINK PANTHER FILM'S -
WITH PETER SELLARS AS THE BUNGLING 'INSPECTOR CLOUSSEAU'

'WHAT'S NEW PUSSYCAT' ALSO STARRED PETER SELLARS
WITH WOODY ALLEN AND PETER O'TOOLE

'THE GRADUATE' WAS DITHERING DUSTIN HOFFMAN
AND ANN BANCROFT AS THE SEDUCTIVE 'MRS.ROBINSON'

WALT DISNEY'S - 'MARY POPPINS' -
FEATURING DICK VAN DYKE AND JULIE ANDREWS

SINGING 'CHIM CHIM CHEREE' &
'SUPERCALIFRAGILISTICEXPIALIDOCIOUS'

DISNEY'S 'THE JUNGLE BOOK' WITH SENSATIONAL SONGS TOO
LIKE 'THE BARE NECESSITIES'
AND "WANNA BE LIKE YOU HOOO! HOO!"

THOSE EXCITING WAR FILMS -
'THE GUNS OF NAVARONE', 'THE GREAT ESCAPE',
'THE BATTLE OF THE BULGE', WE WOULD INDULGE

'THE DIRTY DOZEN',' THE LONGEST DAY'
 AND 'SINK THE BISMARCK' -
(I THOUGHT THAT WAS SOMETHING MI MOTHER DID
WHEN SHE WASHED MI UNDIES IN THE SINK!)

WE SAW CLINT EASTWOOD IN 'WHERE EAGLES DARE'
LESLEY THOMAS'S 'THE VIRGIN SOLDIERS',
'PLAY DIRTY' WITH MICHAEL CANE

THE SATIRICAL 'OH, WHAT A LOVELY WAR!'
WHICH FEATURED BEATLE - JOHN LENNON
(APART FROM THE 'BEATLE FILMS' - NEVER ACTED NO MORE)

'THE WAR GAME' CONTROVERSIAL NUCLEAR DOCUMENTARY
THAT SCARED THE SHIT OUT OF US C.N.D SUPPORTERS
VERY DISTURBING AND SCAREY

AND THOSE GOOSEBUMPING, KNEE TREMBLING, SCAREY, HAIRY
FILMS LIKE - 'THE BOSTON STRANGLER' WITH TONY CURTIS
'PSYCHO' WITH ANTHONY PERKINS AS NORMAN BATES

'THE NANNY' WAS THE EVIL BETTE DAVIES
WHO WAS JUST AS EVIL TO JOAN CRAWFORD IN
'WHATEVER HAPPENED TO BABY JANE' - WERE INSANE!

'LORD OF THE FLIES' - SPOTTY TEENAGE SCHOOLKIDS
MAROONED ON A DESERTED ISLAND -

TURNING TRIBAL, SADISTIC & BARBARIC TO SURVIVE
SCAVENGING AND SAVAGING TO KEEP THEMSELVES ALIVE

'ENDLESS NIGHT' WIH HAYLEY MILLS & 'SCHIZO' HYWEL BENNET
ALFRED HITCHCOCK'S 'THE BIRDS' - WAS UNCANNY

IT MADE YOU THINK TWICE - ABOUT GOING PASSED THE PIGEONS
IN PICCADILLY GARDENS WITH YOUR GRANNY!

'THE GORGON', 'GODZILLA' AND 'THE NIGHT OF THE LIVING DEAD',
'THE MUMMY'S SHROUD' AND 'THE CURSE OF THE MUMMY'S TOMB',
'THE PLAGUE OF THE ZOMBIES' GAVE YOU NIGHTMARES IN BED

'DANCE OF THE VAMPIRES' AND 'DRACULA, PRINCE OF DARKNESS'
'DRACULA HAS RISEN FROM THE GRAVE',
'THE REVENGE OF FU MANCHU'- WITH CREEPY CHRISTOPHER LEE

'THE MASQUE OF RED DEATH' AND 'WITCHFINDER GENERAL'
STARRED THE VERY SINISTER VINCENT PRICE
ALSO WITH CHRISTOPHER LEE

THE SATANIC FILMS LIKE -
DENIS WHEATLEY'S 'THE DEVIL RIDES OUT'

WITH THAT BLACK MAGIC CIRCLE SCENE - THE ANGEL OF DEATH
THAT MADE YOU GASPED FOR BREATH

'DR. FAUSTUS' & 'ROSEMARY'S BABY'
WITH MIA FARROW AS ROSEMARY

CINEMAS WE FREQUENTED IN THE CITY CENTRE
WERE 'THE THEATRE ROYAL', 'THE GAUMONT',
'THE ODEON', 'THE NEW OXFORD'

AND 'DEANSGATE A, B & C'S -
WITH THOSE TWIN SEATS AT THE BACK
WHERE YOU COULD HAVE A GOOD OL' GROPE AND NECK!

AND THE MUCKY - 'THE CINEPHONE'
JUST OFF MARKET STREET
WHICH WAS A 'DIRTY WHITE RAINCOAT'S' PARADISE!

THAT FEATURED ALL THOSE SEXY FRENCH
AND SWEDISH FILMS
FOR PUNTERS LIKE -

OLD JUDGES, SOLICITORS, MINISTERS,
HEADMASTERS, EVEN VICARS! -
SO CALLED PROFESSIONAL PEOPLE

THAT PREACHED ABOUT MORALITY IN THE CITY -
WHAT A SURPRISE!

AND THOSE MIDNIGHT MOVIES -
IN WHICH YOU EITHER FELL INTO
A DRUNKEN SLEEP HALF-WAY THRO'

(OR SNOGGED THE LIPS OF YOUR GIRLFRIEND
ON THE BACK SEAT ALL THE WAY THRO')

THEN YOU WONDER WHY
IN FUTURE YEARS

WHEN SEEING THOSE OLD SIXTIES FILMS
- YOU COULDN'T REMEMBER THE ENDINGS

ALSO IN THE SIXTIES -
YOU HAD FILMS THAT WENT

FROM A HAPPY ENDING
TO A SAD ENDING
TO A NEVERENDING......

ASHTON PALAIS

ASHTON PALAIS WAS ANOTHER GREAT VENUE
THAT FEATURED ALL THE TOP ARTISTS LIKE -

'THE MINDBENDERS' (MINUS WAYNE!)
SINGING THEIR LATEST NO.1 HIT 'A GROOVY KIND OF LOVE'

SOUL SINGER 'LEE DORSEY' -
"WORKIN' IN A COALMINE - GOING DOWN DOWN"
WAS ANOTHER TOP LINER

AND 'THE WHO' - WHO'S SHEER POWER
HAD THE DANCEFLOOR RATTLING & VIBRATING

TO 'SUBSTITUTE', 'I'M A BOY', 'MY G G G GENERATION'
'PICTURES OF LILY' & 'WON'T GET FOOLED AGAIN'

WITH ROGER DALTREY'S FAMOUS MIKE SWINGING
HIGH UP IN THE AIR & CATCHING IT EVERYTIME

PETE TOWNSEND'S - MID-AIR SPLITS
& SMASHING HIS GUITAR TO BITS

KEITH MOON (THE LOON)-
ATTACKING THOSE SKINS -
HITTING THEM WITH ALL HIS MIGHT

JOHN ENTWISTLE THUMPING HIS BASS
THEY WERE RIGHT IN YER FACE -
AN AWESOME SIGHT!

"SUBSTITUTE MY COKE FOR GIN -
I LOOK ALL WHITE BUT MY DAD WAS BLACK
I CAN SEE RIGHT THRO' YOUR PLASTIC MAC"

"I'M A BOY - MY NAME IS BILL & I'M A HEAD-CASE
THEY PRACTICE MAKIN' UP ON MY FACE"

"WHY DON'T YOU ALL FFFFFADE AWAY -
NOT TRY & DIG WHAT WE ALL SSSSSAY"

WE WERE SHAKIN' & GIRATIN' FROM OUR TOES TO OUR FINGERTIPS
THUS EMPTYING OUR BEER GLASSES -
BEFORE THEY TOUCHED OUR LIPS ......

THE TWISTED WHEEL

SATURDAY NIGHT 'ALLNIGHTERS'
WITH GREAT BLUES ARTISTS,
LIVING LEGENDS LIVE AT THE 'WHEEL'
DARK, DANK AND SEEDY,
WITH GREAT D.J.'S LIKE DAVE LEE TRAVIS
WHAT AN ATMOSPHERE - IT WAS UNREAL

YOU JUST SAUNTERED IN, TO THE SLEAZY SOUND
OF 'GREEN ONIONS' BY 'BOOKER T AND THE M.G.'S'
THE EXOTIC 'WOOLY BULLY' BY 'SAM THE SHAM AND THE PHAROES'
OR THE SEXY 'SHE'S ABOUTTA MOVER' BY 'SIR DOUGLAS QUINTET'

ALL THOSE NARROW PASSAGEWAYS WITH LITTLE ALCOVES INBETWEEN
IT WAS LIKE ALLADIN'S CAVE! -
WHERE YOU COULD TRAP, ENSNARE AND SNOG YOUR CAPTIVE ONES
AND GET UP TO ALL KINDS OF MISCHIEF WITHOUT BEING SEEN

I REMEMBER SNOGGIN' THIS GIRL CALLED CLAIRE
TO THE STONES "TELL ME YOU'RE COMIN BACK TO ME"
FOR ABOUT 10 MINUTES OR SO WITHOUT COMIN' UP FOR AIR

ANOTHER BIT OF MISCHIEF WAS SAYING TO A GIRL YOU FANCIED
"I BET YOU THRE'PENCE THAT I CAN KISS YOU ON THE LIPS
WITHOUT TOUCHING YOU - THEN GIVING HER A BIG SMACKEROO

SMILE, FLICK HER THE COIN, SAYING "HERE THAT WAS WELL WORTH IT"
LEAVING HER ALL FLUSTERED WITH A BIG 'CHERRY ON'
IN WHICH SHE WOULD REPLY "YAH! CHEEKY BUGGER, YOU"

LAID BACK AND LISTENING TO 'COUNTRY LINE SPECIAL'
BY THE LATE GREAT LEGENDARY 'CYRIL DAVIES'

"YOU'VE GOT DIMPLES IN YER JAW" AND "BOOM!, BOOM!, BOOM!, BOOM! -
GONNA SHOOT YER RIGHT DOWN", GRUNTED BLUES LEGEND 'JOHN LEE HOOKER'
AND 'THE SPENCER DAVIES GROUP', WITH 'MUFF' AND STEVIE WINDWOOD

"SMOKESTACK LIGHTNING - WHY DON'TCHA HEAR ME CRY
A WHOOO! HOOO! A WHOO! HOO! HOO! HOO! A WHOO! HOOOOO!"
BY 'HOWLIN' WOLF'

"PUT ON YOUR RED DRESS BABY - 'COS WE'RE GOIN' OUT TONIGHT -
PUT ON THOSE HIGH HEEL SNEAKERS" TEASED TOMMY TUCKER -
"WEAR THAT WIG HAT ON YOUR HEAD - WELL ALRIGHT"

WE SAW LEGENDARY BLUES MOUTH HARPISTS LIKE
'SONNY BOY WILLIAMSON THE 2nd' &
'SONNY TERRY' (WITH BROWNIE MAGHEE)'

PLUS LOTS OF BRITISH R & B ARTISTS LIKE -
'JOHN MAYALL'S BLUESBREAKERS'
FEATURING ERIC 'SLOWHAND' CLAPTON - COOL GUITARIST

'ALEXIS CORNER', 'BLUES INCORPORATED',
'JIMMY POWELL & THE 5th DIMENSION'
'THE GRAHAM BOND ORGANIZATION',
'THE DOWNLINERS SECT',
'DUSTER BENNET' (ONE MAN BAND),
'THE VICTOR BROX BLUES TRAIN',
'THE CLIMAX CHICAGO BLUES BAND'

'LONG JOHN BALDRY & THE HOOCHY, COOCHY MEN'
'THE SAVOY BROWN BLUES BAND',
'THE JOHN DUMMER BLUES BAND'
'THE ALEX HARVEY BAND'
THAT WOULD SENT THE TREND

'GEORGIE FLAME AND THE BLUE FLAMES' -
"I SAY YEH! YEH! THAT'E WHARRA SAY - I SAY YEH! YEH!
IN HIS SLEEZY STYLE OF BRITISH JAMAICAN 'BLUEBEAT'

'THE PEDDLERS' JAZZ STYLED COMBO - "LET THE SUN SHINE IN"
"LOUIEE LOUIE OH! BABEE WE'VE GORRA A GO - HI! YI! YI! YI!"
SANG 'THE KINGSMEN' LAID BACK AND KIND OF OFF BEAT
AMERICAN FOLK SINGER 'BOB DYLAN' "CORRINA - CORRINA"

PURPLE HEARTS AND BROWN BOMBERS WOULD FREQUENTLY APPEAR
BUT US LADS WOULD SOONER GO TO 'THE NAG'S HEAD'
OR 'THE (HOUSE OF) RISING SUN' FOR A QUICK BEER

WE USED TO GET THE BACKS OF OUR HANDS RUBBER STAMPED
FOR PASSOUTS TO THE PUBS
THEN YOUR MATE WOULD PRESS HIS HAND ONTO YOURS
('COS THE INK WAS STILL WET!)

THEN CASUALLY STROLL INTO THE 'WHEEL'
FOR FREE - WHAT A SCAM!
IT WORKED FOR A WHILE OUT OF TRUST -
 UNTIL WE EVENTUALLY GOT SUSSED......

THE FREE TRADE HALL

WHERE WE SAW GREAT BLUES CONCERTS
THAT FEATURED BLUES LEGENDS –

'JIMMY REED', 'JOHN LEE HOOKER',
'BIG JOE WILLIAMS', 'T-BONE WALKER',
'LITTLE WALTER' & 'BIG WALTER (SHAKEY) HORTON'

'DUSTER BENNET' (ONE-MAN-BAND)
'CHICKEN SHACK', 'JOHN MAYALL'S BLUESBREAKERS'
WITH ERIC SLOWHAND CLAPTON
WE WERE 'WHOOPIN' & HOLLERIN' WITH
'SONNY TERRY & BROWNIE MAGHEE'

WE EXPERIENCED THE UNIQUE GUITAR
PLAYING OF 'PETER GREEN'
& HIS 'FLEETWOOD MAC' BLUES BAND

EVEN THE GREAT B.B. KING WAS
IN AWE OF HIM BY ANNOUNCING HIM
"AS THE MAN WHO SCARES
THE SHIT OUT OF ME".

WE SAW FOLK HEROES –
'THE DUBLINERS'
& 'STEELEYE SPAN'
WITH THE MAJESTIC 'MARTIN CARTHY'

PLUS CLASSICAL JAZZ ARTISTS –
'THE JACQUES LOUSSIER TRIO'
SPANISH FLAMENCO GUITARIST –
'MANITAS DE PLATAS'

& LEST WE FORGET MODERN JAZZ ELITE
–'THE DAVE BRUBECK QUARTET'

ALSO 'BOB DYLAN' DID HIS INFAMOUS
CONCERT HERE ADMIST THE ANGRY
FOLK PURISTS SHOUTS OF 'JUDAS'
'COS HE WENT 'ELECTRIC' TO PROGRESS

B.B. KING

HEAVEN & HELL

WAS A DARK, DISMAL, DEN OF INIQUITY
IN THE SEEDY PART OF THE CITY
THAT ALSO HAD ALLNIGHTERS -

WITH BLEARY EYES AND LONG MATTED HAIR
AND LITTLE COLOURED LAMPS EVERYWHERE
LOTS OF BLUES BANDS PLAYED THERE

ONE NIGHT IT GOT RAIDED FOR DRUGS
THE POLICE - WOULD YOU BELIEVE ACTUALLY
BROUGHT EXTENSION LADDERS & 200W LAMPS
- TO LIGHT UP THE CLUB

THEN WITNESS THINGS LIKE -
THREE NAKED BODIES EMERGING FROM ONE SLEEPING BAG

PLUS DRUGS OF ALL DENOMINATIONS -
UPPERS AND DOWNERS, REEFER JOINTS, SPEED
PURPLE HEARTS, BROWN BOMBERS ANYTHING YOU NEED

WHAT A DIVE! - AND IT WAS CRAWLING WITH SPIDERS AND BUGS
DROP OUTS AND SPACED OUT PALE FACED MUGS......

TIMES THEY ARE A-CHANGIN'

BOB DYLAN WAS OUR ULTIMATE FOLK HERO
WITH HIS HEAD SCRATCHIN',
SEARCHIN', MINDBLOWIN' LYRICS

WE WERE TRANSFIXED,
HYPNOTISED, ENIGMATIZED

BUT WHEN HE WENT 'ELECTRIC'
AT THE 'MANCHESTER FREE TRADE HALL'

A LOT OF HIS DIE HARD FOLK PURIST FANS DESERTED HIM
WALKING OUT OF HIS CONCERT - CALLING HIM 'JUDAS'
BUT TO US STREETIES - HE WAS IDOLISED

"HOW DOES IT FEEL TO BE ALL ALONE
LIKE A COMPLETE UNKNOWN - JUST LIKE A ROLLIN' STONE"
- WAS LIKE A BLOODY HYMN!
EVEN FELLOW 'FOLKSTER' JOAN BAEZ WAS IN AWE OF HIM

HE WAS PURE POETRY, A GENIUS, THE MESSIAH
SO INFLUENTIAL - HE MADE US STOP, QUESTION AND THINK
ESPECIALLY WHEN YOU SMOKED A JOINT
AND HAD A LARGE 'SPIRITUAL' DRINK!

"I AINT' GONNA WORK ON MAGGIE'S FARM NO MO"
"ALL I REALLY WANNA DOOO! IS BABY BE FRIENDS WITH YOU"

"IT'S ALL RIGHT MA! - I'M ONLY SIGHIN!"
'POSITIVELY 4th STREET', 'IT'S ALL OVER NOW, BABY BLUE'

"IT'S A HARD RAIN - THAT'S GONNA FALL"
"THE ANSWER MY FRIEND IS BLOWIN' IN THE WIND
 THE ANSWER IS BLOWIN' IN THE WIND"

"COME ON WITHOUT, COME ON WITHIN
 YOU'LL NOT SEE NOTHIN' - LIKE THE MIGHTY QUINN"
"EVERYBODY MUST GIT STONED"

 YES HE 'BROUGHT IT ALL BACK HOME' FOR US
 AS WE SANG HIS SACRED SONGS LIKE -
'SUBTERRANEAN HOMESICK BLUES'

 AND "HEY! MR.TAMBOURINE MAN - PLAY A SONG FER ME"
ON THAT ALL NIGHT, MIDNIGHT 216 BUS......

BOB DYLAN

END OF THE WORLD (ACCORDING TO LEONARD COHEN)

AT THE END OF A RELATIONSHIP
WHEN YOU'RE FEELING DOWN, DEPRESSED AND MANIC

YOU WOULD LISTEN, ALONE AND IN PAIN
TO THE SAD (VERY SAD) SONGS OF 'LEONARD COHEN'

SONGS LIKE -
"SUZANNE TAKES YOU DOWN TO HER PLACE NEAR THE RIVER"
AND "SO LONG MARIANNE, IT'S TIME WE BEGAN
TO LAUGH AND CRY, LAUGH AND CRY ABOUT IT ALL AGAIN"......

THE MANCHESTER CAVERN/MAGIC VILLAGE

WAS IN CROMFORD COURT, JUST OFF MARKET STREET
WITH THE RESIDENT D.J. DAVE LEE TRAVIS

WHERE THE CONDENSATION DRIPPED
OFF THOSE SWEAT SOAKED, SALT CELLAR WALLS
ADMIST THE HEAT, HUMIDITY & CLAMMINESS

BUT IT DIDN'T BOTHER US CRAZED KIDS
AS THE ADRENALINE PUMPED OUT OF OUR SWEATY BODIES
- IT WAS SHEER EXCITEMENT AND BLISS

"GIRL YOU REALLY GOT ME GOIN' -
YOU GOT ME SO I DON'T KNOW WHAT I'M DOIN'"
ROCKED RAY DAVIES'S KINKS

"THERE SHE WAS JUSTA WALKIN' DOWN THE STREET
SINGIN' DO WAH DIDDY DIDDY DUM DIDDY DOO"
SANG MANFRED MANN'S PAUL JONES - RATTLIN' HIS MARACAS

IT WAS A SUPERB VENUE, APART FROM THE LOO -
THAT SMELT A BIT LIKE BELLE VUE ZOO......

MAGIC VILLAGE

FEATURED PROGRESSIVE GROUPS LIKE -
THE EDGAR BROUGHTON BLUES BAND
CHANTING - "OUT! DEMONS! OUT!"

MARC BOLAN'S TYRANNOSAURUS REX
SINGING "RIDE A WHITE SWAN - DA DA DEE DUM DUM"
AND "OH! DEBORRRAAH - YOU LOOK LIKE A ZEBRRRAA"

THE INCREDIBLE STRING BAND
(OR AS WE WOULD JEST - THE INCREDIBLE STRING VEST)
AND LOTS OF OTHER UNDERGROUND SOUNDS

AND THAT HEADY AROMA OF JOS STICKS & CANNABIS
Will REMAIN WITH ME FROM THAT DAY 'TIL THIS......

SOUL NIGHT'S IN RAINY CITY

DISCO-TAKIS, PLACEMATE 7, THE JIGSAW, ROUNDTREES SOUND,
TIME & PLACE, GUYS & DOLLS, MR. SMITHS, THE BLUENOTE,
THE CAN CAN & TOP OF THE TOWN –
WERE THE FINEST SOUL CLUB'S AROUND

BLUE & BRONZE MOHAIR SUITS,
RED BRACES, TRILBY'S, CROPPED HAIR
A BLUE & WHITE SPOTTED TIE & MATCHING HANKY –
YOU WERE IN THERE!

"MY NAME'S AL CAPONE, DON'T ARGUE" SANG PRINCE BUSTER –
"CHIC A BUM! CHIC A BUM!" AS WE SHUFFLED TO SKA
"I'M A SOUL MAN", "SOUL SISTER BROWN SUGAR",
SANG SAM & DAVE & "HOLD ON I'M COMING"

"I'M A ROADRUNNER BABY" –
WE WERE "SHAKE & FINGERPOPPIN"
TO JUNIOR WALKER & THE ALL STARS

"MUSTANG SALLY - HUH!"
AND "I'M GONNA WAIT 'TIL THE MIDNIGHT HOUR"
ROARED WILSON PICKETT WITH SOUL POWER

WHILE OTIS 'MY GIRL' OTIS REDDING WAS
"JUST SITTING AT THE DOCK OF THE BAY"
LISTENING TO MARVIN GAYE
SING "I HEARD IT THROUGH THE GRAPEVINE"

AS LEE DORSEY WAS "WORKIN' IN A COALMINE
GOIN' DOWN, DOWN"
& THE ISLEY BRO'S "THIS OL' HEART OF MINE"

WE WERE ASSURED THAT "EVERYTHING WAS ALRIGHT,
UPTIGHT - OUTTA SIGHT"–
AS WE BOOGIED WITH STEVIE WONDER TO GREAT DELIGHT

"LIKE A SEX MACHINE" SCREAMED SEXED UP SOUL KING JAMES BROWN
"IT'S A MAN'S WORLD", "PLEASE, PLEASE, PLEASE",
& "PAPA'S GORRA BRAND NEW BAG - OWW!"

'KNOCK ON WOOD' KNOCKED EDDIE FLOYDD
& "WAR HUH! WHAT IS IT GOOD FOR? ABSOLUTELY NOTHING"
AS WE WERE SMOOCHIN' & SNOGGIN' TO PERCY SLEDGE'S –
"WHEN A MAAAAN LOVES A WOMAN" & "WARM & TENDER LURRVE"
JIMMY RUFFIN'S "WHAT BECOMES OF THE BROKEN-HEARTED
WHO HAVE LOVED AND NOW DEPARTED –
I KNOW I'VE GOTTA FIND, SOME KINDA PIECE OF MIND -BA-A-BEE!"

WE HAD 'STAX' AND 'MOTOWN' IN THE SOUL'S OF OUR BROGUE'S
AS WE SHUFFLED ON DOWN TO THE FOUR TOP'S -
"SUGAR PIE HONEYBUN - I KNOW WHEN YOU ASKED ME TOO,
I CAN'T HELP MYSELF, I LOVE YOU AND NOBODY ELSE"

AND "DARLIN' REACH OUT, REACH OUT FOR ME -
JUST LOOK OVER YOUR SHOULDER -
COS I'LL BE THERRRRE TO LOVE AND CHERISH YOU"

"IT TAKES TWO BABEE - ME AND YOU" -
 A SOUL SEARCHIN' DUET EMBRACED BY MARVIN GAYE & KIM WESTON
- "TO MAKE A DREAM COME TRUE"

"HOW SWEET IT IS TO BE LOVED BY YOU" SMOOCHED MARVIN GAYE
SOMETIMES WHEN YOU WERE SAD AND FEELING DOWN
YOU'D MOPE AND SOB TO SMOKIE ROBINSON AND THE MIRACLES
"THE TRACKS OF MY TEARS" AND "TEARS OF A CLOWN"

AND "OOH! BABY I'M LOSING YOU" AND "BALL OF CONFUSION"
FROM THE TITANIC TEMPTATIONS - WE WERE UNDER NO ILLUSION!
AS WE MARVELLED, DREAMILY TO THE MARVELETTES -
"WHEN YOU'RE YOUNG AND IN LOVE"

AND DANCED SEXILY TO JOHHNY TAYLOR'S "WHO'S MAKING LOVE"
AND WHEN GLADY'S KNIGHT & THE PIPS
WERE "LEAVIN' ON THAT MIDNIGHT TRAIN TO GEORGIA"

WE WERE "DANCIN' IN THE STREET"
WITH MARTHA & THE VANDELLAS
"OOOOO OO OOH! BABY LOVE",

"SET ME FREE, WHY DON'TCHA BABE -
YOU JUST KEEP ME HANGIN' ON"
AND "I'M GONNA MAKE YOU LOVE ME"
SANG THE SEXATIONAL SUPREMES

THOSE TANTILISING TAMS WITH
"HEY GIRL DON'T BOTHER ME"
AS FONTELLA BASS PLEADED "RESCUE ME"
MARY WELLS WAS LOOKING FOR "MY GUY"

ALL ARETHA FRANKLYN WANTED WAS "A LITTLE RESPECT"
"AWWW!! - SHOW ME A MAN THAT'S GORRA A GOOD WOMAN -
NOW SHOW ME?" BOASTED JOE TEX

THESE MAGIC SOUL SINGER'S WERE SHEER CLASS
"DO YAH! LIKE GOOD MUSIC" - SCREAMED ARTHUR CONLEY -
"HUH! THAT SWEET SOUL MUSIC - OH! YEH! OH! YEH!"

AS WE "DANCED TO THE MUSIC" WITH SLY & THE FAMILY STONE
SINGING "PAPA WAS A ROLLIN' STONE" - WE WERE NOT ALONE!
"THEY WERE DANCING IN CHICAGO - DOWN IN NEW ORLEANS
EVEN IN THE MOTOR CITY" - AND ESPECIALLY OUR RAINY CITY

YES! THESE WERE THE SOUL NIGHT'S IN RAINY CITY
SOUL NIGHT'S IN 'THE LAND OF A THOUSAND DANCES'
IN THE TOWN OF A THOUSAND PUDDLES......

PHIL SPECTOR

THE PHIL SPECTOR 'WALL OF SOUND'
CREATED SOME OF THE BEST MUSIC AROUND

'YOU'VE LOST THAT LOVIN' FEELIN'
BY THE RIGHTEOUS BROTHERS

AND 'UNCHAINED MELODY'
APPEALED TO ALMOST EVERYONE INCLUDING OUR MUM!

IKE AND TINA TURNER'S 'RIVER DEEP MOUNTAIN HIGH'
WAS SO POWERFUL - IT MADE GROWN MEN CRY!

THE CRYSTALS 'TIL I KISSED HIM'
AND 'DA DOO RON RON'

THE 'RONETTES 'BE MY BABY'
AND 'BABY I LOVE YOU'
TURNED YOU ON! ON! ON!

BURT BACHARACH

(WITH HAL DAVID)

SENT 'MESSAGES TO MARTHA'
AND 'MESSAGES TO MICHAEL'
VIA 'TRAINS & BOATS & PLANES'

HE CREATED MANY HITS FOR -
SENSATIONAL SINGER - DIONNE WARWICK
LIKE 'DON'T MAKE ME OVER' AND 'ANYONE WHO HAD A HEART'
WHICH WAS ALSO A MASSIVE HIT FOR CILLA BLACK

SANDIE SHAW '(THERE'S) ALWAYS SOMETHING THERE TO REMIND ME'
HE ALSO HAD A GREAT MUSICAL SOUND
THAT FEATURED IN SOME THE BEST SEX AROUND......

CABARET

GREAT CABARET CLUB'S LIKE - THE DOMINO & THE PRINCESS,
WHISKY A-GO-GO', THE NORTHERN & SOUTHERN,
OCEANS 11 & POCO-A-POCO

THE CROMFORD CLUB, DENO'S & THE WARREN
TALK OF THE NORTH & THE GOLDEN GARTER -
WITH SHEP'S BANJO BOYS JUST FOR A STARTER!

TOP LINERS APPEARED LIKE -
CATHY KIRBY, BRUCE FORSYTH,
TOMMY COOPER, NORMAN WISDOM

BOB MONKHOUSE, AL READ,
LULU, DUSTY SPRINGFIELD
TOMMY STEELE, FRANKIE VAUGHAN & DAVID WHITFIELD

LOCAL BLUE COMEDIANS LIKE PAT MILLS, AL SHOWMAN,
JACKY CARLTON, JOHNNY GOON-TWEED & BERNARD MANNING

GREAT SINGERS LIKE -
EX -'DRIFTERS' - BEN E. KING
AND SOLOMAN KING - "SHE WEARS MY RING"

COMEDY ACTS LIKE -
THE BARON KNIGHTS, THE BLACK ABBOTS, THE GRUMBLEWEEDS
AND CANDLEWICK GREEN WITH THEIR BIG HIT -
"WHO DO YOU THINK YOU ARE,
YOU'VE TRIED TO PUSH ME A BIT TOO FAR"

EVERY ACT SEEMED TO FINISH OFF THEIR SETS
WITH EITHER 'UNCHAINED MELODY',
"IT'S O-O-ONLY MAKE BELLLL-IEVE"
OR "YOU'LL NNNNNEVERRRR WALLLLLK AAAALONE"

THEN THERE WAS THE DEVONSHIRE IN ARDWICK GREEN
THAT USED TO ENTICE A CERTAIN TYPE OF DRAG QUEEN
LIKE BUNNY LEWIS AND FRANK FOO FOO LAMAR

AND ENTERTAIN CAMP AND SAUCY PANTOMIMES
LIKE 'PUFF IN BOOTS', 'CINDERFELLA',
'BABES IN THE NUDE', 'ALADDIN IN DRAG'

AND 'TURN AGAIN - DICK WHITTINGTON' (THE MIND BOGGLED!)
FULL OF INNUENDOS, VERY FUNNY,
LEWD & EVER SO SLIGHTLY CRUDE

I REMEMBER SEEING - BILL HALEY & THE COMETS
AT THE BROADWAY CLUB IN FAILSWORTH
SUPPORTED BY 'THE SWINGIN' BLUE JEANS'

WITH MY GIRLFRIEND LYNN,
THAT WAS ONE HELL OF A SHOW -

"GET READY! - ON YER MARKS! LET'S GO! MAN GO!"
AS WE "SHAKED, RATTLED & ROLLED" ALL THE WAY HOME......

FAGINS

THE COMPERE WAS CALLED JOHNNY MARTIN
WHO ALWAYS SANG GENE PITNEY NUMBERS LIKE
24 HOURS FROM TULSA, BACK STAGE
AND I'M GONNA BE STRONG (WITH THE BIG FINISH!)

HE WOULD GET STAG & HEN PARTIES VICTIMS UP ON STAGE
TO SAY CHEEKY RHYMES LIKE "ONE SMART FELLOW' HE FELT SMART,
TWO SMART FELLOWS THEY BOTH FELT SMART"

AND "I'M NOT A PHEASANT PLUCKER,
I'M A PHEASANT PLUCKER'S SON
AND I'M ONLY PLUCKING PHEASANTS
'TIL THE PHEASANT PLUCKER COMES"

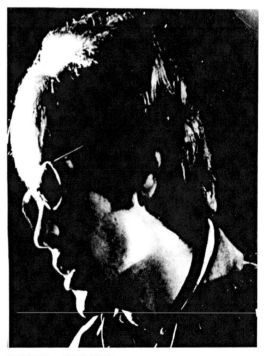

IT ALSO FEATURED FINE ARTISTS
LIKE SCOTT WALKER -
WITH HIS SUPERB BARITONE VOICE
SINGING SONGS LIKE JOANNA,
THE LIGHTS OF CINCINATTI,
MONTAGUE TERRACE IN BLUE,

AND THE HAUNTING, DAUNTING SONGS OF
JACQUES BREL LIKE - JACKIE,
AMSTERDAM & MY DEATH
WHICH SENT CHILLS DOWN YOUR SPINE
THAT ALMOST CUT YOU IN TWO.....

SCOTT WALKER

OTHER CITY CLUBS

YOU HAD GUYS & DOLLS,
THE BODEGA, MR.SMITHS
THE NOTORIOUS NILE CLUB

THOSE MECCA DANCE HALLS –
THE PLAZA AND THE RITZ

AND YOU'D HAVE AN ABSOLUTE BALL
AT THE NEW CENTURY HALL

AND IF YOU COULD SWIVEL THOSE HIPS –
YOU COULDN'T FAIL
AT THE BROOKE BOND NATIONAL
TWIST & TWITCH CHAMPIONSHIP
HELD AT THE LOCARNO, IN SALE

FOR AN EXPRESSO, OR CAPPUCCINO
YOU DIDN'T HAVE TO VENTURE FAR
TO THE CONA, KARDOMAH OR MOGAMBO COFFEE BAR

FOR A CHEAP NIGHT OUT - THE CATACOMBS
THE NEW AMBER MOON, THE HOUSE OF BAMBOO
THE FORTY THIEVES AND THE BACK DOOR

OUT OF TOWN CLUBS LIKE –
THE BONEYARD IN BOLTON
THE RICHMOND CLUB IN ROCHDALE

BAILEYS IN OLDHAM,
THE CANDY CLUB, THE KOHL CELLAR,
AND SINATRA'S CLUB IN FAILSWORTH

PLUS MANY MANY MORE......

THE RITZ

THIS WISE OL' MAN ONCE SAID TO ME -
THAT YOU CAN'T BEAT THE OL' BIDDIES COS
THEY DON'T YELL, THEY DON'T TELL AND THEY DON'T SWELL

SO ME AND MY MATE ARRIVE ANXIOUSLY AT
THE MOULIN ROUGE OF MANCHESTER - THE RITZ
ON GRAB A GRANNY NIGHT - WHAT A NIGHT!

AFTER TRIPPING A LIGHT FANDANGO
OVER THIS BID'S HANDBAG - ON MY DANCE FLOOR DEBUT
AND BURNING HER ARM WITH A SENIOR SERVICE CIG

TO A RESPONSE OF SHEER VENOM THAT WENT SOMETHING LIKE
"SSSHIT!! WATCH OUT YAH! 'EFFIN', STUPID CLUMSY PIG!"

THUS GETTING THE INEVITABLE K.B. (KNOCK BACK)
THEN TRYING TO REGROUP
AFTER CALLING FOR A COMB THROUGH AND A PEE

WE THEN VENTURED INTO THE BARGAIN BASEMENT
AND LAUGHED AT ONE POOR SOUL
WITH A WALNUT WHIP TYPE HAIRSTYLE (COMBED BACK TO FRONT)

COS WHEN HE JIVED -
HE ENDED UP LOOKING LIKE THE PHANTOM OF THE OPERA
MIND - I THINK HE WAS DANCING WITH ONE OF DRACULA'S BRIDES?

AS BETTY THE BLOW UP DOLL LOOKALIKE
BOBBLES HER BOBBLIN' BOOBS AROUND THE DANCE ARENA
HARRY THE HASBEEN SWOOPS LIKE A VULTURE PREYING ON CARRION

RETALIATES BY THRUSTING HIS THIGHS,
GYRATING AND SWIVELLING HIS SNAKE HIPS -
LIKE A POOR MAN'S TOM JONES
THIS HAD BETTY LICKIN' HER RUBY RED LIPSTICK LIPS

HIS ROUGH-AS-A-BEARS-ARSE IMAGE
IMPRESSES HIS OVER-HEATED, ANXIOUS PREY
HE THEN SETS TO WORK ON BODY LANGUAGE AND FOREPLAY
OR HIS TACKY TECHNIQUE OF HOW TO HAVE A QUICK LAY

SITTING ALL GOOEY-EYED IN A LITTLE ALCOVE
AFTER A FEW CHERRY B'S
FOLLOWED BY A GOOD OL' RAUCOUS SNOG
BETTY DISAPPEARS DEEP INTO THE LADIES BOG

AFTER SOMETIME, SUBMERGES WEARING FRESH TUTTY
TICKS HARRY OFF FOR BEING SMUTTY
HARRY'S OVER-REACHIN' THIGH BOUND HAND
GET'S A LITTLE GIGGLE FOLLOWED BY A SMACK

"I'M NOT THAT SORT OF GIRL!" LIES BETTY
THEN PROCEEDS TO UNDO HER ZIP AT THE BACK
JUST AS HARRY STARTS TO CURSE
SHE INDIGNANTLY WHISPERS - "TOP!! FIRST"......

BLACKPOOL

EASTER WEEKEND TRIPS TO BLACKERS
IN CAR LOADS WE VENTURED WITH GREAT PRIDE
TO OUR FAVOURITE NORTH WESTERN SEA-SIDE
IN MY MATE RAY'S SINGER GAZELLE

WITH DAVE MAC, DAVE ROB HIS BRUV ARNIE, SYD, SOL & SKELL
DOIN' A TON WAS FUN - BUT IT WOULD RATTLE LIKE HELL

IN A CERTAIN GUEST HOUSE –
"THERE WERE EIGHT IN A BED
AND THE DRUNKEN ONE SAID ROLL OVER, ROLL OVER
'TIL ONE ROLLED OVER AND ONE FELL OUT
ONE STAGGERED UP AND GAVE ONE A CLOUT"

AFTER HAVIN' A FEW IN THE MANCHESTER ARMS
WE'D STAGGER IN FILE
ALONG THE INFAMOUS GOLDEN MILE
PASSING BETWEEN CALLS INTO THAT
CORAL ISLAND RIP OFF AMUSEMENT ARCADE

ICE CREAM, CANDY FLOSS, TOFFEE APPLES, SUGAR DUMMIES
KISS-ME-QUICK HATS & NAME RIGHT THRO' ROCK STALLS

SNIGGERING AT THOSE SAUCY MUCKY POSTCARDS ON THE WAY –
LIKE THE ONE WITH AN OUTSTRECHED HAND HOLDING A PAIR
OF KNICKERS FROM THE SIDE OF THE STAGE CURTAINS
SHOUTING TO THE UNFORTUNATE ICE SKATER DOIN' A TWIRL
"HEY SONIA!" WITH THE LOOK OF SHEER EMBARRASSMENT
FROM THE BLUSHING YOUNG GIRL

ONE GULLIBLE WOULD STOP AT FORTUNE TELLER –
'GYPSY ROSIE LEE' – "CROSS MI PALM WITH SILVER DEAR"
"BUGGER THAT!" SAY'S SOL – "LET'S GO FER ANOTHER BEER"

SAT SINGIN' & HUMMIN' THE TURTLES SONG 'SO HAPPY TOGETHER'
THE BOX TOPS 'THE LETTER' ON THE JUKEBOX IN THE TOWER BAR
PLAYING SNOOKER & DARTS WAS LIKE THE THIRD WORLD WAR

THEN WE'D RUN FULLY CLOTHED INTO THAT TURD INFESTED SEA
TRYING TO RIDE THAT BUCKING BRONCHO WAS A SIGHT TO SEE
THEN ONTO THE PLEASURE BEACH AND BIG RIDES –
TURNING GREEN ON THE GRAND NATIONAL ROLLER COASTER RIDE
THEN WHITE ON THE BIG WHEEL, WALTZER AND GHOST TRAIN

YOUR WORLD TURNED UPSIDE DOWN ON THAT HAUNTED SWING
TESTING YOUR MUSCLE ON THAT STENGTH MACHINE
YOU HIT WITH A BIG MALLET TO MAKE THE BELL RING
THEN OFF TO THE FUN HOUSE
ROLLIN' THRO' THOSE REVOLVING BARRELS
CLINGIN' DESPERATELY TO THAT WALL OF DEATH

SLIDIN' BY THE SKIN OF YOUR ARSE
DOWN THEM ALMOST VERTICAL BIG SLIDES
WHAT EXCITEMENT - WHAT A FARCE!

THEN IT WAS OFF TO THAT LITTLE CAFÉ
THAT READ JUGS OF TEA & SAND
WITH THE LETTERS 'WICHES' MISSING FROM THE END
MADE US CHUCKLE, "AYE! IT WERE REET GRAND"……

THE LAKES

CAMPING IN 'AMBLESIDE'
AFTER HITCHING A RIDE

WE PITCHED OUR TENTS
IN A FARMER'S FIELD
WE OFTEN USED AS THE GENTS

BEING AKIN
WITH NATURE
WAS A SHOCK
TO US TOWNIES

ALTHOUGH WE SOMETIMES
BEHAVED LIKE
FARM ANIMALS

WE WERE WILD & FREE
UNDER CANVAS
OVER THE LEA

HAVING GREAT BANTER
WITH OTHER CAMPERS
THIS WAS THE LIFE
FOR MY MATES & ME

I REMEMBER US
INTERLOPERS BEING
CHASED FROM THE LOCAL
VILLAGE DANCEHALL

BY THESE JEALOUS GUYS
AFTER FLIRTING WITH
THEIR GIRLFRIENDS

WE HAD TO CLIMB OUT
OF THE TOILET WINDOW
& ONTO THE RICKERTY ROOF,
TO ESCAPE AND GET AWAY

- LIVING EXTREMELY DANGEROUS FOR A DAY......

ISLE OF MAN (65)

SAILING ON THAT 'MANX MAID'
ACROSS THAT ROUGH, RETCHING, IRISH SEA
TO THE I.O.M. HOLIDAY CENTRE IN DOUGLAS

SINGING THE BEACH BOY'S "WE SAILED ON THE SLOOP JOHN B"
WERE MY MATES - DAVE SEMPLE, JIMMY PIFCO, BARRY BOOTH & ME

'I GOT YOU BABE' WAS No.1 SUNG BY SONNY & CHER
WITH THEIR WEIRD, WAY OUT CLOTHES & FREAKY HAIR
"HANG ON SLOOPY, SLOOPY HANG ON" SANG THE McCOYS

"WILD THING - YOU MAKE MY HEART SING -
YOU MAKE EVERY THING GGGROOVEEE!"
WAILED THE TROGGS AND US WILD BOYS

INSPIRED BY THE NEW BEATLES MOVIE 'HELP!'
AND EMULATING OUR HERO'S - BY RUNNING WILD & FREE
INTO THE POURING RAIN ACROSS
THAT HALF DESERTED DOUGLAS BEACH
LEAP FROGGIN' OVER EACH OTHER,
WADING FULLY CLOTHED INTO THAT MAD IRISH SEA

NIGHTS WERE SPENT BETWEEN THE MERMAID & VILLA MARINA
AND INBETWEEN CHRISTINE, PAM AND TINA
(GIRLS WE PULLED FROM STOCKPORT)

ONE NIGHT WE ALL WENT TO
SEE MANFRED MANN
AT THE FAMOUS DOUGLAS PALACE -
IT WAS 'PAUL JONES'S' FAREWELL
CONCERT -
 A GREAT NIGHT! SINGING APTLY -
"IF YOU'VE GOTTA GO, GO NOW OR
ELSE YOU'VE GOTTA STAY ALL NIGHT"

I REMEMBER THIS HOLIDAY
AS IF IT WERE YESTERDAY
WHEN ALL MY TROUBLES
SEEMED SO FAR AWAY
AS WE SAILED BACK HOME SADLY
IN THAT 'YELLOW SUBMARINE'
(WE WISHED)
AFTER RETCHIN' & RIFTIN' AGAIN
ON THAT SEA-SICK, SEA-SICK SEA......

GET YOUR KICKS IN YEAR 66
(ALL THIS & ENGLAND WINNING THE WORLD CUP)

WE WERE JUST 'LAZING ON A SUNNY AFTERNOON' (THE KINKS)
CHILLIN' OUT WITH A COUPLE OF DRINKS
SHARING 'SUMMER IN THE CITY' (LOVING SPOONFUL) SUCH A PITY

BECAUSE ON 'MONDAY MONDAY' (MAMMAS & PAPPAS)
I SAID MY LAST GOODBYE'S TO MY GIRLFRIEND 'SUE'
WHO WAS EMIGRATING WITH HER FAMILY TO AUSTRALIA
THE LAND OF THE KANGEROO, KOALA & DIDGERIDOO

WE KISSED & SMOOCHED TO DUSTY SPRINGFIELD'S -
'YOU DON'T HAVE TO SAY YOU LOVE ME'
"I CAN'T LET GO" (THE HOLLIES) SAY'S I WITH A TEAR IN MY EYE

TO MY LOVELY 'ELUSIVE BUTTERFLY OF LOVE' (BOB LIND)

"YOU ARE 'MY GIRL' (OTIS REDDING)

AND I AM YOUR 'SUNSHINE SUPERMAN' (DONOVAN)

NOT ANY OLD 'DAY TRIPPER' (THE BEATLES)
YOU SEE "THIS GUY'S IN LOVE WITH YOU" (HERP ALBERT)
YOU SIGH & SAY THAT "YOU'RE OUT OF TOUCH MY BABY" (CHRIS FARLOW)
AND THAT "THESE BOOTS ARE MADE FOR WALKIN'" (NANCY SINATRA)

I REPLY JUST "GIMME SOMMA LOVIN" (SPENCER DAVIES GROUP)
BEFORE YOU "KEEP ON RUNNIN' - RUNNING FROM MY ARMS"
WE ARE LIKE TWO "STRANGERS IN THE NIGHT" (FRANK SINATRA)

"WE CAN WORK IT OUT" (THE BEATLES) SOMEHOW?
"LIFE IS VERY SHORT FOR FUSSING & FIGHTING MY FRIEND"
& THAT "I WANT TO SPEND MY LIFE WITH A GIRL LIKE YOU"(THE TROGGS)
COS YOU'RE SUCH A 'WILD THING', A 'PRETTY FAMINGO' (MANFRED MANN)

OH! "GOD ONLY KNOWS WHAT I'D BE WITHOUT YOU" (THE BEACH BOYS)
AND "THE SUN AIN'T GONNA SHINE ANYMORE" (THE WALKER BRO'S) FOR ME
ALTHOUGH I'M FEELING DOWN, "I'M A BELIEVER" (THE MONKEES)
THERE ARE STILL 'GOOD VIBRATIONS' (THE BEACH BOYS) IN THE AIR

SO JUST "REACH OUT & I'LL BE THERE" (THE FOUR TOPS)
"WHEN I WOKE UP THIS MORNIN'
- YOU WERE ON MY MIND"(CRISPIAN ST.PETERS)

AS I LISTENED SADLY TO 'GUANTANAMERA' (THE SANDPIPERS)
AND 'THE SOUND OF SILENCE' (SIMON & GARFUNKEL) ALL ALONE

I WAS 'WISHING & HOPING' WITH SUCH 'SORROW' (THE MERSEYS)
THAT SOMEDAY YOU'D RETURN TO THE –
'GREEN, GREEN GRASS OF HOME' (TOM JONES)

I WAS TO BECOME A 'PAPERBACK WRITER'
LOOKING FOR 'MY MICHELLE', MY 'ELEANOR RIGBY'

& 'YESTERDAY'
WAS JUST A
FADED MEMORY

AS FOR THE
FUTURE
WELL 'TOMORROW
NEVER KNOWS'
(THE BEATLES)

SO LET'S JUST
"TURN OFF
YOUR MIND
RELAX & FLOAT
DOWN-STREAM,

IT IS NOT DYING
IT IS NOT DYING
(THE BEATLES)

FOOTY

IN THE SIXTIES TWO OF THE MOST EXCITING FOOTBALLING MOMENTS
OF MY LIFE OCCURED - ENGLAND HAD WON THE 'WORLD CUP' IN 66'
AGAINST WEST GERMANY 4 - 2 AT WEMBLEY
(WITH A TERRIFIC 'HAT TRICK' FROM - GEOFF HURST)

AND MY TREASURED TEAM MAN. UNITED HAD EVENTUALLY
WON THE 'EUROPEAN CUP' IN 68' 4 - 1 AGAINST FAVOURITES
BENEFICA ALSO AT WEMBLEY - WHAT A DECADE!

THERE WAS A GREAT BUZZ EVERYWHERE
(APART FROM SCOTLAND 66' AND MAINE ROAD 68' OVER THERE!)

ALEX STEPNEY- THE HERO -
WITH HIS SUPERB LAST MINUTE SAVE FROM THE GREAT EUSABIO

SHAY BRENNAN, TONY DUNNE, BILLY 'COWBOY' FOULKES,
PADDY CRERAND, NOBBY 'THE ASSASSIN' STILES, DAVID SADLER,

LOCAL LAD JOHNNY ASTON - WHO PLAYED THE GAME OF HIS LIFE,
ALSO ANOTHER LOCAL 'BABE' BRIAN KIDD (KIDDO)
WHO HEADED A SUPER GOAL ON HIS 19th BIRTHDAY WHAT A MOMENTO!

CAPT. BOBBY CHARLTON WHO SKIMMED THE FIRST GOAL IN
OFF HIS SHINEY HEAD AND BLASTED HIS SECOND GOAL IN THE
USUAL INIMITABLE CHARLTON STYLE - TOP CORNER OF THE NET

AND 'EL BEATLE' THE GREAT GENIUS GEORGIE BEST -
WHO STARTED THE RIOT WHEN HE ROUNDED THE KEEPER
IN EXTRA TIME -
AN AMBITION ACHIEVED FOR SIR MATT!

WE WERE IN AWE! -
AND YOU HAD TO FEEL FOR THE 'INJURED' DENIS LAW
MISSING OUT ON SUCH AN HISTORIC OCCASION

EVEN RIVALS MAN.CITY HAD A DECENT TEAM IN THE SIXTIES
AND THEY WON THE 'EUROPEAN CUP WINNER'S CUP' IN 1970
2 - 1 AGAINST POLISH SIDE GORNIK ZABRE IN VIENNA

WITH GOALSCORER'S NEIL YOUNG AND FRANNY LEE - PENALTY!
GREAT PLAYER'S LIKE COLIN BELL, MIKE 'BUZZER' SUMMERBEE,

MIKE DOYLE, GLYN PARDOE, AND FRANCIS (DIVER) LEE,
THE CREAM OF CITY
SUCH EXCITEMENT WERE THE LOCAL DERBY'S IN THOSE DAYS
YOU WOULD ARGUE FOR WEEKS ON END
ABOUT BESTY AND BELL'S BLISTERING DISPLAYS

GREAT PLAYERS OF THIS ERA -

SAFE AS BARCLAYS 'GORDON BANKS', GENIAL 'GEORGE COHEN',
RACING 'RAY WILSON', THE BATTLING 'ALAN BALL',
MIGHTY 'MARTIN PETERS',
THE PULSATING POWER OF 'BOBBY CHARLTON'
AND HIS BROTHER THE GIRAFFE BIG 'JACK CHARLTON',
RAMPANT 'ROGER HUNT', HATRICK HERO 'GEOFF HURST',
CAPT.COOL 'BOBBY MOORE', SMILING ASSASSIN 'NOBBY STYLES'
AND THE GREAT GOAL SCORING 'JIMMY GREAVES' -
WERE THE STARS OF ENGLISH FOOTBALL

SCOTLAND'S - SWIVEL HIPS 'JIM BAXTER',
MASTER PASSER 'PADDY CRERAND'
BRAVE HEART 'BILLY BREMNER',
THE MIGHTY 'DAVE MACKAY',
THE SLICK 'IAN ST.JOHN',
LITTLE GINGER WINGER 'JIMMY JOHNSTONE'
AND THE BLOND 'KING' HIMSELF 'DENIS LAW' WERE TOP DRAW

NORTHERN IRELAND'S - GENIUS 'GEORGE BEST'
AND BIG BUCKET HANDS 'PAT JENNINGS'

EIRE'S - GREAT VISIONARY THE STYLISH 'JOHNNY GILES'
AND DASHING 'DANNY BLANCHFLOWER'

WALES'S - BIG JOHN CHARLES
AND THE MIGHTY IVOR ALLCHURCH

AND THE FANTASTIC FOREIGNERS LIKE BRAZIL'S -
THE BLACK PEARL 'PELE' AND THE LITTLE BIRD 'GARRINCHA',
THE PORTUGESE POWERHOUSE 'EUSABIO',
THE BLACK FLASH RUSSIAN GOALKEEPER 'YASHIN',
THE CLASSY WEST GERMANY CENTREBACK 'BECKENBAUER',
HUNGARY'S GREATEST 'PUSKAS',
THE SPANISH SPEED KING 'GENTO' AND DEVASTATING 'DI STEFANO'

AND YOU WOULD FIND THEM ALL -
LOITERING IN 'CHARLES BUCHAN'S' FOOTBALL ANNUALS I RECALL......

BOXING

CASSIUS CLAY - LATER MOHAMMED ALI
BEAT SONNY LISTON FOR THE WORLD HEAVY-WEIGHT TITLE IN 63'
'FLOAT LIKE A BUTTERFLY & STING LIKE A BEE'
& ' I AM THE GREATEST' & WE'D ALL AGREE
UNTIL HE WAS KNOCKED DOWN BY OUR 'ENNEREE'
UNFORTUNATELY HE GOT BACK UP & THE REST IS HISTOREEE!!

WRESTLING

AT THE KINGS HALL - BELLE VUE
WITH JACKIE PALLO (HURRAH!) v MICK McMANUS (BOO!)
GREAT CHARACTERS LIKE LES KELLET & BIG DADDY

THE TAG TEAMS - THE FEARLESS DUO'S
THE ROYLE BRO'S & THE PYE BRO'S
GIANT HAYSTACKS COLOGNE WHO WAS ABOUT SEVEN FOOT TWO
THE 'HEADBUTTING' MASK & COUNT BARTELLI WERE THE BEST
THEY NEVER LOST A CONTEST

BILLY TWO RIVERS WITH HIS MOHICAN HAIR STYLE
KENDO NAKASAKI CLAD IN LEOPARD SKIN FURS
SUAVE STEVE MILLER, WILD JIM HUSSY, MASAMBULA
JOHNNY KWANGO, VIC FAULKNER, TIBOR ZACHAS
WOULD ENTERTAIN THE LOT OF US……

ASHTON COLLEGE (HALF TERM)

LOTS OF PARTYING, WILD, WILD TIME
GIRLS ON THE PILL, WHAT A THRILL!

WE EVEN HAD PARTIES AT THE LOCAL REVERAND'S FLAT
REV. NEIL HANLEY - AN ECCENTRIC CHARACTER

WHO USED TO BUSK AROUND THE TOWN
HE RESIDED IN ASHTON-U-LYNE - HE WAS SOUND!

HE WOULD PLAY HIS GUITAR, SING & SQUAT
AS WE LISTENED AND JOINED IN THE CHORUS'S
- ABOUT TWENTY FOUR OF US

WE WERE PROMISCUOUS AND BED HOPPING WAS IN FASHION
LOTS OF LUST AND HOT TEENAGE PASSION

AS IF IT NEVER HAPPENED BEFORE
(ESPECIALLY ON THE REVERAND'S FLOOR)

PETE & ANNA, NICK & ANNA, KEITH & EDWINA
ART STUDENTS THAT MET UP VIA ASHTON COLLEGE

AND I ALSO HAVE FOND MEMORIES OF LETTING THE NEW YEAR IN
WITH MY BLOND POLISH GIRLFRIEND NINA

MAKE LOVE! - NOT WAR!
WAS JUST THE EXCUSE WE WERE LOOKIN' FOR......

HIPPY DAZE

WHAT A LAUGH AND A LARK -
WATCHING MY MATE KEITH MANNING
WADING THROUGH THE LAKE IN HIS GIRLFRIENDS DRESS

COMPLETE WITH BEADS AND HEADSCARF
IN ASHTON-U-LYNE'S STAMFORD PARK

WE WERE DRESSED AS HIPPIES –
KEITH, NICK HOMOKI, THE GIRLS AND ME
GIVING OUT FLOWERS AND BLOWING KISSES

AMUSING THE STUDENTS
AND UPSETTING THE LOCAL THUGS
WHO CALLED US CISSIES

THEN THESE LOCAL THUGS
PROCEEDED TO CHASE AFTER US
WE RAN LIKE HELL AND LEFT THEM FOR DEAD

'TIL THEY JUMPED IN A VAN
AND LEFT US FOR DEAD INSTEAD

ABOUT TEN OF THEM PILED OUT
PLUS THIS ENORMOUS GUY
CALLED 'BIG BILL' OF ASHTON

WHO APPARENTLY WAS ASHTON'S
CHIEF OF POLICE'S WAYWARD SON
HE WAS AS BIG AS A BUS
AND KICKED THE HELL OUT OF US

BUT FORTUNATELY WE HAD A WITNESS,
& WE TOOK THEM TO COURT
FOR SUSPENDED SENTENCES......

FLOWER POWER (1967)

THOSE HAIRY, HEDONISTIC, HALCYON DAYS
OF LOVE, PEACE, HIPPIES, HOPE AND HAPPINESS
LOVE BEADS, BANDANAS AND KAFTANS
CANNABIS KISSES ON L.S.D. LIPS

AS WE DANCED AND PRANCED ENCHANTEDLY
TO THE BEATLES, BEACH BOYS, BYRDS, BOB DYLAN, FREE
THE STONES, WHO, TEN YEAR'S AFTER WITH ALVYN LEE

"IF YOU GO TO SAN FRANCISCO,
WEAR SOME FLOWERS IN YOUR HAIR"
SANG SCOTT MACKENZIE WHO WAS RIGHT ON IN THERE!

AND THE FLOWERPOT MEN'S –
"LET'S GO TO SAN FRANCISCO WHERE THE FLOWERS GROW"

FRANK ZAPPA AND THE MOTHERS OF INVENTION,
JOHN SEBASTION'S LOVING SPOONFUL, KING CRIMSON,
CROSBY, STILLS, NASH AND YOUNG, THE GRATEFUL DEAD

THE DOORS, JEFFERSON AIRPLANE,
BUFFALO SPRINGFIELD, COUNTRY JOE AND THE FISH
BLODWYN PIG, JANIS JOPLIN & THE BIG BROTHER HOLDING COMPANY
AND OUR ULTIMATE HERO'S THE JIMI HENDRIX EXPERIENCE

THE VELVET UNDERGROUND, LOVE, SANTANA,
JOE COCKER AND HIS BIG GREASE BAND

WE WERE SINGING JEFF BECK'S - 'HI HO SILVER LINING'
WITH OUR HEART'S BEATING AND EYES SHINING
'I CAN HEAR THE GRASS GROW' SANG THE PSYCHEDELIC MOVE –

WE WERE MOVED! ESPECIALLY TO PINK FLOYD'S 'ARNOLD LANE'
TRAFFICS 'HOLE IN MY SHOE' THE BEATLES DOUBLE SINGLE –
'STRAWBERRY FIELDS FOREVER' AND 'PENNY LANE'

"STANGE BREW" STIRRED CLAPTON'S CREAM –
"GIRL WHAT'S INSIDE OF YOU"
AS THE STONE'S SEDUCTIVELY SANG 'DANDELION' & 'WE LOVE YOU'

1969 WAS THE YEAR OF THE WONDEROUS 'WOODSTOCK ROCK FESTIVAL'
THROUGH RAINSTORMS AND MUD,
HALF A MILLION PEOPLE WERE IN ABSOLUTE ECSTACY

"WE ARE STARDUST WE ARE GOLDEN
AND WE HAVE GOT TO GET OURSELVES BACK TO THE GARDEN"

THE THEME SONG WRITTEN BY 'JONIE MITCHELL'
AND SANG SEDATELY BY MATTHEWS SOUTHERN COMFORT

THE BEATLES MASTERPIECE 'SARGEANT PEPPER' ALBUM
WITH HALLUCINATING TRACKS LIKE -
'LUCY IN THE SKY WITH DIAMONDS'(LSD?)

'A DAY IN A LIFE' AND "FOR THE BENEFIT OF MR. KITE
- THERE WILL BE A SHOW TO-NIGHT"

FROM EASTERN CULTURES AFAR -
CAME 'RAVI SHANKAR' EMBRACING HIS SITAR

THE MARAHISHI YOGI'S - TRANSCENDENTIAL MEDITATION
CONTEMPLATION OF ONE'S NAVEL - A NEW SPIRITUALIZATION

AS WE "TIPTOED THROUGH THE TULIPS" WITH TINY TIM

TRIPPING, STRIPPING AND DANCING STARK-NAKED
WITH THE 'SUSIE CREAMCHEESES' - AT A WHIM!

WE WERE FAR OUT! FREAKED OUT! TURNED ON!
PSYCHEDELIA - LOVE IN'S - MAN WE WERE SOLID GONE

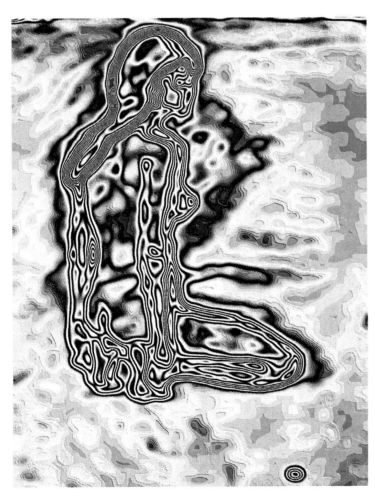

IN A CRYSTAL MAZE
AS WE TRANSCENDED
INTO THE
'PURPLE HAZE

TURNING
A 'WHITER SHADE
OF PALE'
WITH L.S.D. & ALE

WE WERE AS HIGH
AS 'MR.KITE' -
OUR FIRE WAS ALIGHT!

"ALL YOU NEED
IS LOVE -
LOVE IS ALL
YOU NEED"
WAS THE SEED

MAKE LOVE - NOT WAR!
TURN ON! TUNE IN!
AND DROP OUT!......

COLLEGE OF COMMERCE

COLLEGE OF COMMERCE, AYTOUN STREET JUST OFF PICCADILLY
FRIDAY NIGHT'S - STUDENT NIGHT'S

WITH RESIDENT GROUP - 'BARCLAY JAMES HARVEST'
SINGING THEIR HIT
 "SO YOU WANNA BE A ROCK AND ROLL STAR -
GONNA MAKE IT ON YOUR OWN"

YOU HAD 'THE MOODY BLUES' ON ONE NIGHT
SINGING THEIR BIG CHART HIT - 'NIGHT'S IN WHITE SATIN'
AND SONGS FROM THEIR ALBUMS - 'ON A THRESHOLD OF A DREAM'
AND 'DAY'S OF FUTURE PAST'- THEY WERE SUPREME

I REMEMBER 'THE NICE' WITH KEITH EMERSON
ATTACKING, SLASHING AND STABBING HIS ORGAN

(HIS ELECTRIC ONE OF COURSE) LIKE HE WAS POSSESSED
(OR JUST PLAINLY PISSED)
PLAYING THEIR VERY FAST VERSION OF "DA DA DA DA IN AMERICA"

'JOE COCKER AND HIS BIG GREASE BAND'
GROWLIN' & GRUNTING HIS MASSIVE HIT
'WITH A LITTLE HELP FROM MY FRIENDS'

- PLAYING HIS IMAGINARY GUITAR
WITH HIS SLIGHTLY DISTORTED
'LEMON SUCKIN' FEARSOME FACE
AND HIS HANDS & ARMS FLAYING ALL OVER THE PLACE
'THE HUMBLE BUMS' WERE FOLKSTERS -
FEATURING GERRY RAFFERTY
AND THE VERY FUNNY - BILLY CONNOLLY

THEY HAD BIG SCREEN'S PLAYING 'LAUREL AND HARDY'
AND 'THE KEYSTONE COPS' TYPE OLD MOVIES EVERYWHERE
LOTS OF BAR'S AND DANCEFLOOR'S
AND HAIRY, HIPPY & STUDENTY TYPES HANGIN' IN THERE......

MARKET STREET, MANCHESTER 1963

DIRTY OL' TOWN

SATURDAY NEET'S AT THE M.S.G. FOLK CLUB
NEAR VICTORIA STATION & THE MANCHESTER ARMS -
(WHICH WAS THE CITY'S OLDEST PUB)

"NNYYYYYAAAAA!!!!" GRIMACED THE BEARDED, POT-BELLIED SINGER
WI' FINGER IN TH'EAR & T'OTHER HAND CLENCHING A PINT O' BEER
AS WE JOINED IN THE 'WILD ROVER' CHORUS OF -

"NO NAY NEVERRRR! NO NAY NEVERRR NO MORRRRE -
WILL I PLAY THE WILD ROVERRRR, NO NEVERRR NO MORRRRE"
SINGIN' OUR HEART'S & BEERY 'YED'S OFF -
'TIL WE ALL FELL RAT-ARSED OUT OF TH' DOOR

WE SANG SONG'S LIKE EWAN McCOLL'S 'DIRTY OL' TOWN' -

"I MET MY LO O O O VVVE BY THE GAS WORK'S CCCCROFT
DREAMED A DREAM BY THE OL' CANAAAAL -
KISSED MY GIRL AT THE FACTORY WALL
DIRTY OL' TOWN, DIRTY OL' TOWN"

LOCAL SINGER'S LIKE MIKE HARDING, MARY ASQUITH,
MARIE LITTLE & PETE SMITH -"YE MARINER'S ALL AS A YOU WALK
BY - COME IN AND DRINK IF YOU ARE DRY"

PETE ROYLE, TONY DOWNS, HARRY BOARDMAN WITH HIS -
"UP A LADDER, DOWN A WALL, TU'PENCE & THRE'PENCE -
GOD BLESS US ALL"

PAUL READ - "WHAT HAVE YOU BEEN DOING IN THE WOODS ALL DAY
HENEEERY MY SON? - EATING EEL'S DEAR MUVER -
EEEEL'S!!! DEAR MUVER - OH! MUVER BE QUICK
'COS I WANNA BE SICK, AN' LAY ME DOWN TO DIE"

AEMON & GERRY WITH THE BEGGARMEN -
"MRS MAGRAAA' LIVE'S ON THE SEA-SHORE"
AND "I AM A JOLLY BEGGARMAN" -
WHICH HAD US JIGGIN' & REELIN' ALL OVER THE ALE SODDEN FLOOR

OWDAM TINKER'S SINGING THEIR MELODY -
"UP! UP! TO TH' BUTCHER'S SHOP
I DARE NOT STAY MUCH LONGER
FER IF I DO, MI MUTHER WILL SAY -
I'VE BEEN PLAYING WIV GIRL'S DOWN YONDER'
EARLIE! IN THE MORNIN', - EARLIE! IN THE MORNIN'
BEFORE THE BREAK OF DAY"
AND "EEH! BY GUM, AINT' IT FUN -
SHOOTIN' PEAS UP A NANNY GOAT'S BUM"

WE SAW CLASS SINGER'S LIKE MARTIN CARTHY
SING 'HIGH GERMANY' AND 'GENTLEMAN SOLDIER'
THE GREAT EWAN McCOLL & PEGGY SEGER SINGING -
'THE FIRST TIME EVER I SAW YOUR FACE' IN PERFECT HARMONY

ACE GUITARISTS BERT JANSCH 'ANGIE'
AND JOHN RENBOURNE 'THE WALZ' ACE GUITARISTS
HAMISH HIMLACH WITH HIS BIG JELLY, BELLY LAUGH
THE WIT OF ALEX CAMPBELL & NOEL MURPHY WITH MANDOLIN PLAYER
'SHAGGIS' (DAVY JOHNSTONE) WHO LATER JOINED ELTON JOHN
PAUL SIMON (BEFORE HE BECAME INCREDIBLY FAMOUS)

CHRISTY MOORE - "WHO WAS DAT DER TO TICKLE DA TOE'S OF ME -
ONLY MISSUS CUNAH - CUNAH! DEAR DON'T COME ANY NEAR TO ME"

FOLK & BLUES ARTISTS LIKE 'BOTTLE NECK' SLIDE GUITARIST -
STEPHEN GROSSMAN - WHO THREW HIS OCCASIONAL 'TANTRUM'
WHEN BEING INTERRUPTED PLAYING HIS FAMOUS RIFF'S
- A REAL PERFECTIONIST

JOANNE & DAVE KELLY WITH THEIR RENDITIONS OF -
'BARREL HOUSE BLUES' WITH BOOGIE-WOOGIE PIANIST BOB HALL

ALSO CHAMPION JACK DUPREE WAS A REAL CHARACTER
IF YOU WENT FOR A PEE IN THE NIGHT -
HE WOULD SING EMBARRASSINGLY- "I KNOW WHERE YER GOIN'-
I KNOW WHERE YER GOIN'- I HOPE EVERYT'ING COME OUT AWRIGHT!"

THE HUMBLEBUMS WITH BILLY CONNOLLY WERE AS USUAL HILARIOUS
THE NONE SMOKIN' NONE DRINKIN' AL STEWART WHO'S ONLY VICE
WAS TO BE THE FIRST FOLKSTER TO USE THE 'F' WORD ON RECORD)

MOST OF THESE ARTIST'S PLAYED AT THE
'CAMBRIDGE ANNUAL FOLK FESTIVAL' WITH TOP LINERS LIKE -

THE DUBLINER'S, MAGNA CARTA, THE YOUNG TRADITION,
THE IAN CAMPBELL FOLK GROUP, THE McCALMANS,
THE FUREYS, THE JOHNSTONS,
THE CLANCEY BRO.'S WITH TOMMY MAKIN,

RALPH MCTELL, ROY HARPER, JOHNNY SILVO, MICHAEL CHAPMAN,
DAVIE GRAHAM, JOHN FAHEY, GORDON GILTRAP,
SPIROGYRA, PENTANGLE, BOB DAVENPORT, PLANXTY,
SWEENEY'S MEN & STEELEYE SPAN

WE'D ALL TRUNDLE OFF IN OUR MATE 'MALC'S MINI VAN
ABOUT HALF A DOZEN OF US YOUNG FOLKSTER'S
ALL CRAMPED UP LIKE SOZZLED SARDINES IN A BEER CAN

AT CAMBRIDGE BOTH INSIDE & OUTSIDE THE MARQUEE'S
WE'D SQUAT, CROSSLEGGED & JOIN IN THE CHORUS'S

LOTS OF THE ARTISTS WERE JAMMING WITH EACH OTHER
LIKE THE DUBLINER'S FAMOUS LUKE KELLY & RONNIE DREW
(WHO BOUGHT US ALL A PINT TOO!)

AND IN THE MISTY MORNING, ADMIST THE GRUNTING & GROANING
WE'D ALL EXPERIENCE SUCH KING SIZE HANGOVER'S
AND PLEAD WITH 'THE LORD ABOVE' PLEASH HIC! OH! PLEASH GOD
PLEASE VANQUISH ALL MORNIN' AFTERS THE NIGHT BEFORES......

BILLY CONNOLLY

SATURDAY NIGHT 'HEAVER'

COLLAPSE ON THE BED - A TERRIBLE MESS
A GOOD NIGHT WITH THE LADS - THEN YOU UNDRESS
BETWEEN THE SHEETS - FISSED AS A PART HIC!
AND THAT IS WHEN IT'LL START
THAT DREADFUL, SWIRLING, WHIRLING PIT
OH! NO! YOU CRY - OH! SHIT!

AROUND AND AROUND
SWIRLING AND WHIRLING
SPINNING AND TURNING
YOUR BRAINS WILL GO
MOANING AND GROANING

YOU START TO PRAY
(IN A HYPOCRITICAL WAY)
OH! GOD! PLEASE GOD! NO!

SLIDE OUT OF BED
ON ALL FOURS YOU CRAWL
LEGLESS TO THE BATHROOM FLOOR
ARM 'ROUND THE TOILET - HEAD IN THE BOWL

COUGHIN' AND SPITTIN'
YOUR EYES START TO ROLL
RETCHIN' AND RIFTIN'
HEAVIN' AND HONKIN'
PUKIN' AND SPEWIN'

UP COMES YOUR DINNER AFTER YOUR TEA
TOMATO SKINS AND CARROTS
PLUS THE OCCASIONAL PEA!
ASHEN FACED, RED EYED,
A TERRIFIC THROBBIN' HEAD
WISHING YOU WERE BLOODY DEAD

"OHHH! NNNEVER AGAIN,
OHH! NEVER AGAIN"
YOU CROAK AND QUAKE

KNOWING FULL WELL YOU'LL BE
THE SAME NEXT WEEK......

TOSSA DE MAR (1967)

WE MADE OUR FLYING DEBUT -
THE DAY AFTER THE 'STOCKPORT AIR DISASTER'
WHAT A SEND OFF! FOR MY MATE DAVE LITTLER & MYSELF - PHEW!

THE WILSON GOVERMENT ONLY ALLOWED US JETSETTERS
A MISERLY £28 (V FORM AMOUNT!)
TO TAKE OUT OF THE COUNTRY FOR SPENDS

DUE TO THE 'OL TIGHTEN YER BELTS' SITUATION
- SOMETHING TO DO WITH INFLATION

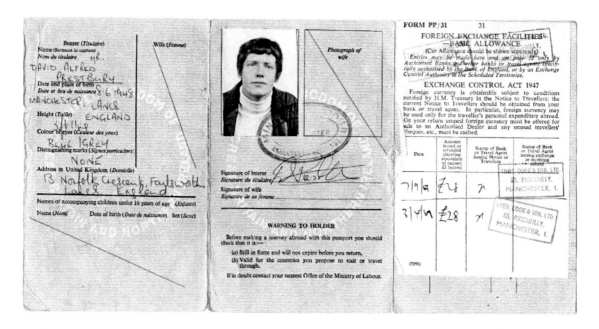

WE FLEW TO GERONA AIRPORT, COSTA BRAVA - VIVA ESPANIA!
AND STAYED AT THE 'HOTEL TERRANOVA'

GOING THROUGH THAT 'PAIN BARRIER' AS FAST AS YOU CAN
TO GET A STINGING, SUNBURNING, REDFACED, RED NOSED SUNTAN

SMOTHERED FROM HEAD TO TOE WITH 'AMBER SOLAIR'
MAKING AQUAINTANCES WITH 'SAN MIQUEL' SPANISH BEER

CHEAP CHAMPAGNE, WHITE BACARDY & SPANISH BRANDY
WE WERE YOUNG, DARING, RAMPANT & RANDY

WENT TO A 'BULLFIGHT' IN BARCELONA ONE NIGHT
SAW 'EL CORDOBEZ' THE FAMOUS MATADOR
YOU CAN SAY BEING ENGLEEESH
WE WASN'T IMPRESSED - TOO MUCHO BLOOD & GORE

HAD A FEW GOOD NIGHT'S IN 'PADDY'S BAR'
SHINGIN' IRISH FOLK SHONGS BY THE SCORE

THEN STAGGERED OUT TO THE NIGHT CLUB 'THE ROCAMAR'
IRONICALLY COPPED OFF WITH A COUPLE OF 'POLICE GIRLS'
FROM SHEFFIELD BACK HOME

WE ALSO HAD A LAUGH & A LARK
WITH A COUPLE OF LIVERPOOL 'JUDIES'
WHO WERE STAYING AT OUR HOTEL

THEY KEPT PLAYING PRANKS ON US BOYS
LIKE SNEAKING INTO OUR BEDROOM & MAKING 'FRENCH BEDS'

ANS PUTTING ALL KINDS OF UNSAVOURY THINGS
UNDER OUR BEDSHEETS TO ANNOY US

ANYHOW! WE GOT OUR REVENGE -
BORROWED THEIR ROOM KEY OFF 'HOSEA'
THE RECEPTIONIST & GOOD FRIEND - 'OLEY!'

WE THEN COLLECTED ALL THEIR KNICKER'S & BRA'S
AND HUNG THEM MISCHIEVOUSLY OVER THE HOTEL 'FLAGPOLE'
WHAT A DISPLAY - TO THEIR DISMAY!

THEY CHASED US ALL OVER 'TOSSA DE MAR' & AFAR
- WITHOUT ANY KNICKER'S & BRA? ......

LLORET DE MAR (1968)

AFTER VENTURING NOT VERY FAR
TO THE NEAREST SPANISH BEACH BAR
WERE MYSELF, DAVE LITTLER, DEN ROBINSON AND BAZ BOOTH

DRINKING LITRES OF 'BACARDY & COKES'
LAUGHING HYSTERICALLY AT SILLY JOKES
I REMEMBER THIS BIG, BIG 'JOHN WAYNE LOOKALIKE' GUY
WHO CAME SWAGGERING UP TO THE BAR

AND IN THE SQUEAKIEST GIRLY VOICE YOU HAD EVER HEARD
LISPED "CAN I HATH A BEER & A BABYSHAM PLEASETH PABLO DEAR?"
WELL WE ALL JUST FELL ABOUT LAUGHING IN HYSTERICS
NEARLY WETTING OURSELVES - WHAT A STAR!

GETTING ABSOLUTELY WRECKED AND THROWING UP
WASN'T BIG AND IT CERTAINLY WASN'T CLEVER
WE HAD TO STAY IN OUR ROOMS AT THE 'XAINE PARK HOTEL'
FOR A COUPLE OF DAYS & NIGHTS TRYING DESPERATELY TO SOBER UP

'DO IT AGAIN' SANG THE BEACH BOY'S IN HIGH REFRAIN
THE LOCALS CALLED US 'EL BEATLES'
REFERRING TO OUR MOP TOP HAIR STYLES
(APART FROM DEN WHO WAS A BIT THIN ON TOP)

'LA BAMBA' & 'GUANTANAMERA' WERE PLAYED IN EVERY SPANISH BAR
'HEY JUDE' BY THE BEATLES WAS THE MOST MEMORABLE SONG
FROM THIS HOLIDAY - THAT MADE US PROUD TO BE ENGLEEESH!
WE USED TO TORMENT THE HOTEL ROOM MAIDS
SAYING THINGS LIKE "YOU SENORA OR SENORITA"

ONE WOULD REPLY "MI SENORA MI THREE BAMBINO'S!!"
THEN I'D SAY "ME AND YOU FOUR BAMBINO'S? - SI!"
THEN SHE WOULD RUN OUT OF THE ROOM
AND CALL ME "MUCHA LOCO! MUCHA LOCO!"
JABBERING ON IN HER SPANISH LINGO

SOME MORNINGS WHEN THEY CAME
IN JABBERING ON -
WE'D ALL STAND THERE STARKERS
PARADING OUR NAUGHTY BITS
AS IF WE HADN'T SEEN THEM -
FOR A BIT OF FUN
THEY WOULD SHRIEK, SCREAM,
DROP THEIR TOWELS AND RUN
INTO THAT SCORCHING HOT, SPANISH, SUNBURNING SUN......

THOSE WERE THE DAYS

68' WAS A GREAT YEAR -
MAN.U. WERE THE FIRST ENGLISH TEAM TO WIN THE 'EUROPEAN CUP'
JUST SEEING THE SHEER DELIGHT ON THE GREAT MATT BUSBY'S FACE
BROUGHT A TEAR TO MANY A MANCUNIAN EYE

'DON PARTRIDGE' - ONE MAN BAND
HAD A COUPLE OF HIT'S WITH "ROSIE OH! OH! ROSIE -
I LOVE TO PAINT YOUR FACE UP IN THE SKY"
AND 'BLUE EYES' THEN DISSAPEARED QUICKLY BACK UNDERGROUND
I REMEMBER HIM BEING INTERVIEWED -
& BEING ASKED THE QUESTION ABOUT HIM NOT READING NEWSPAPERS
"WHAT'S THE POINT IN READING ABOUT SOMETHING
YOU CAN DO ABSOLUTELY NOTHING ABOUT" HE'D INDIGNANTLY SAY

HE WAS A REALLY GENUINE 'SALT OF THE EARTH' TYPE CHARACTER
WHO WENT BACK ONTO THE STREET'S OF LONDON
TO BUSK THE REST OF HIS LIFE AWAY

'THE CRAZY WORLD OF ARTHUR BROWN'
WITH HIS ZANY HIT "FIRE! - I'LL TEACH YOU TO BURN"
HE USED TO WEAR 'FLAMING HEADGEAR' AS PART OF HIS ACT
- ONE NIGHT HE SET HIS HAIR ALIGHT - OHHH! SHITE!

THE BEATLES FABULOUS 'HEY JUDE' WAS A BIG No.1
"NAA NA NA NANA NA NAA" THE BEST ENDING OF A SONG EVER!
ALSO 'THOSE WERE THE DAYS' A SONG 'PAUL McCARTNEY'
ADAPTED FOR 'MARY HOPKIN'
AN 'OPPORTUNITY KNOCKS' WINNER FROM WALES)

'THE BONZO DOG DOO DA BAND' SCORED WITH -
"I'M THE URBAN SPACEMAN BABY - I'VE GOT SPEED
I'VE GOT EVERYTHING I NEED"

'EVERLASTING LOVE' BY LOVE AFFAIR
'BABY COME BACK' BY THE EQUALS
& 'MONY MONY' BY TOMMY JAMES & THE SHONDELLS
ALL GREAT DANCE RECORDS OF THAT YEAR
'JUMPING JACK FLASH' FROM 'THE STONES'
& 'BARRY RYAN'S' 'ELOISE' WERE ROCK CLASSICS

THE DOWN SIDE OF 68' WAS THE ASSASSINATIONS OF -
'MARTIN LUTHER KING' CIVIL RIGHTS CAMPAIGNER
WHO WAS SHOT DOWN IN MEMPHIS
AND SENATOR 'ROBERT KENNEDY' WHO WAS ALSO
GUNNED DOWN IN L.A. TWO MONTHS LATER......

ON THE ROAD AGAIN (1969)

3.56 a.m. B.S.T. ON 21st JULY 1969
WAS MANS HISTORIC FIRST MOON LANDING
'ONE SMALL STEP FOR A MAN, ONE GIANT LEAP FOR MANKIND'

WOW! WHAT A TRIP! HOW HIGH COULD YOU GET?
(MUST HAVE BEEN ON L.S.D. - HOW HIP!)

THIS WAS THE YEAR OF 'CHARLES MANSON'
AND HIS SATANIC DISCIPLES BRAINWASHED WITH EVIL AND HATE

WHO HORRIBLY MURDERED HOLLYWOOD FILM STAR 'SHARON TATE'
AND HER PARTYING FRIENDS

'WOODSTOCK' MUSIC FESTIVAL (A REACTION TO THE VIETNAM WAR)
THE DROWNING DEATH OF 'BRIAN JONES' OF THE ROLLING STONES

I REMEMBER THE 'STONES' HYDE PARK CONCERT
MICK IN MARRIANNES'S DRESS LOOKING A BIT OF A 'NELLY'
READING AN ELEGY FOR BRIAN - BY THE POET 'SHELLEY'

'POP ART' WAS IN VOGUE WITH ANDY WARHOL, DAVID HOCKNEY,
ROY LICHENSTEIN, JASPER JOHNS, TOM WELLSELMANN

AS THE U.S.A'S ART ICONS AND BRITAINS PETER BLAKE -
WHO DESIGNED THE 'COLLAGE' COVER FOR THE BEATLES
'SARGEANT PEPPER' ALBUM IN 1968

ALSO 'OP ART'S BRIDGET RILEY WHO INFLUENCED
THE SIXTIES FASHION
WITH HER BLACK AND WHITE OPTICAL DESIGNS

U.S.A.'S BEAT POET'S LIKE ALAN GINSBERG & FERLINGHETTI
U.K.'S ADRIAN MITCHELL, ADRIAN HENRY, ROGER McGOUGH
AND BRIAN PATTEN FROM LIVERPOOL WERE THE ORDER OF THE DAY

JOHN AND YOKO WERE AN ITEM WITH THEIR 'BAGISM' & 'BED-IN'S'
FOR PEACE - "ALL WE ARE SAYIN' - IS GIVE PEACE A CHANCE"
WAS THEIR PROTEST AND POLITICAL STANCE

1969 WAS ALSO THE YEAR WE HITCH-HIKED ACROSS NORTHERN EUROPE
HOLLAND, BELGIUM, WEST GERMANY AND DENMARK

AFTER SETTING OFF BY FERRY ON ONE WAY TICKET'S
FROM 'HARWICH' TO THE 'HOOK OF HOLLAND'
ALL FEELIN' QUITE QUEASY AND SEA SICK
DUE TO THE VAST CONSUMPTION OF DUTY FREE WHISKEY
THAT WAS READILY AVAILABLE TO DEN, WIGGY, MIKE & ME

WE DECIDED TO SPLIT UP INTO TWO'S - TO GET LIFTS EASIER
THE MASTER PLAN WAS TO MEET UP THE FOLLOWING NIGHT
IN PUTTGARTEN PORT, WEST GERMANY DEN & WIGGY, MIKE & ME

TRAVELLING BY TRAIN FROM HOLLAND WITH DISSENT
AFTER SLEEPING ROUGH BY THE MOTORWAY EMBANKMENT
IN OUR SLEEPING BAGS - WITHOUT A TENT -

'COS WE LEFT IT IN THE FIRST LORRY WE HITCHED A LIFT IN
JUST THE START WE NEEDED -
LIKE SCORING AN 'OWN GOAL' IN THE FIRST MINUTE!

WORSE WAS TO FOLLOW -
DUE TO EXTREME LACK OF SLEEP, WE DOZED OFF ON THE TRAIN
ONLY TO MISS OUR BLOODY STOP IN HAMBURG

WE HAD TO JUMP OFF THE TRAIN AS IT WAS SLOWIN' DOWN
INTO THE NEXT TOWN,
THEN SCUTTLE OVER A LARGE WOODEN FENCE,
AS ANOTHER TRAIN WAS PULLING IN

AND BLOCKING OUT THE STATION MASTER'S VIEW
- RUNNIN' EXCITINGLY LIKE SOMETHING OUT OF
THE 'THE GREAT ESCAPE' WAR MOVIE - PHEW!

WE THEN PROCEEDED TO BAFFLE 'PASSPORT CONTROL'
AS WE WERE CROSSING THE BORDER INTO DENMARK
WITHOUT HAVING OUR PASSPORTS STAMPED

CONFUSING THE OFFICIALS WHO EVENTUALLY LET US THRO'
FOUR DAY'S IT TOOK US TO GET THERE - SOME PLANNING
(AND APPARENTLY WE ONLY JUST MISSED THE OTHER TWO!)

"WHERE DO YOU GO TO MY LOVELY" -
SANG PETER SARSTEDT
"WHEN YOU'RE ALONE IN YOUR BED -
SHOW ME THE THOUGHT'S THAT SURROUND YOU
I WANT TO LOOK INSIDE YOUR HEAD - YES I DO - YES I DO"

AND 'SOMETHING IN THE AIR' WERE MASSIVE HITS THAT YEAR
FOR THUNDERCLAP NEWMAN (WITH THAT FUNNY PIANO BIT!)

THOUGHTS OF 'GET BACK' BY THE BEATLES CROSSED OUR MIND'S
AS OUR RUCKSAC'S LAID HEAVY ON OUR BACKS

SMELLIN' STRONGLY OF WHISKEY
THAT SMASHED INSIDE MIKE'S RUCKSAC
WHEN WE JUMPED FROM THE TRAIN AND OUT OF THE STATION
BUT WE TRUDGED WEARILY ON AND ON

IN DENMARK - WE STOPPED AT A LITTLE VILLAGE CALLED 'MARIBO'
AFTER FIRST MAKING OUR WAY, UNBEKNOWING THRO'
A LUNATIC ASYLUM IN RODBY-HAVN WHICH WAS SLIGHTLY DAUNTING

WE MET UP WITH QUITE A FEW FRIENDLY YOUNG VIKINGS
PER, HELGE, SAUL, YEN, NILGE, JACOB, EVA & ANETTE
STAYED IN PER'S APARTMENT UNTIL THE LANDLORD KICKED US OUT

THEN WE STAYED FOR A FEW NIGHTS
IN JACOBS FATHER'S DOCTOR'S MANSION
(WHO INCIDENTLY WAS ON HOLIDAY WITH HIS MISTRESS FOR A WEEK)
WHERE WE HAD SOME REALLY WILD PARTIES - IT WAS HAUNTING

WE WERE VOLUNTEERED TO BARTER FOR ILLEGAL SUBSTANCES
IN COPENHAGEN'S CENTRE - THE RED SQUARE SOMEWHERE?
(COS BEING EEENGLISH WE COULD GET A GOOD DISCOUNT)

WELL WE CAME BACK WITH A BAGFULL OF BLACK STUFF
THAT LOOKED LIKE OXO CUBES TO US - WHAT A HASSLE
THEN ON TO A PARTY IN 'KNUTHENBORG CASTLE'

HAD AN INCREDIBLY WILD WEEKEND,
SMOKING FROM PIPES AND BONGS
LISTENING TO ROLLING STONES SONGS

GETTIN' ABSOLUTELY STONED AND SPACED OUT
HALLUCINATING AS I KISSED THE BEAUTIFUL BLOND ANETTE
SO OUT OF MY HEAD - I KISSED HER SO HARD HER LIPS BLED
THEN I COLLAPSED ON THIS FOUR POSTER BED

AWOKE WITH TWO DANISH WHIRLS (GIRLS) EVA AND ANNETTE
TRUTH IS THAT I DON'T RECALL THE THRILL OF IT ALL
AND GOD FORSAKEN! IF I EVER GOT MY DANISH BACON

- I FELT I LET OL' ENGLAND DOWN
SAID OUR GOODBYES AND LEFT THE PARTY WITH A FROWN
(LOWERING THE UNION JACK DOWN)

OH! ANNETE - HOW COULD I FORGET HER!
THEN WE LEFT TO HEAD BACK HOME
SINGING SIMON AND GARFUNKEL'S 'HOMEWARD BOUND'

ON ROUTE A 'STRANGER THAT FICTION' HAPPENED TO ME
MIKE AND I SPLIT UP IN COPENHAGEN (TO GET LIFTS MORE EASILY)

I GOT A LIFT IN A MERC OFF AN EXTREMELY NICE AMERICAN FAMILY
ALL THE WAY TO HAMBURG, WEST GERMANY

WANDERING AIMLESSLY THRO' THE 'REEPABAUN' ONE DAY
WITNESSING - A COUPLE OF GUN SHOTS GOING OFF
FROM A STREET FIGHT ACROSS THE WAY
'HMMM! I SUDDENLY THOUGHT - TIME I WAS ON MY WAY!
I EVENTUALLY, AFTER SOME DELAY,
GOT A LIFT RIGHT THRO' TO HOLLAND THEN INTO BELGIUM

AND WAS DROPPED OFF AT THE SIDE OF THE MOTORWAY
THAT WENT TO OOSTEND (OSTEND)
(MY CASHFLOW WAS DEPLETING, SO I DECIDED IT WAS CHEAPER
TO TRAVEL FURTHER DOWN TO BELGIUM RATHER THAN HOLLAND)

ANYHOW - THIS WHITE MINI COOPER SUDDENLY SLOWED DOWN
A GUY WITH LONG BLOND HAIR JUMPED OUT
AND STARTED TO WAVE AND SHOUT LIKE HE WAS DOIN' A WAR DANCE
- IT WAS ONLY MY MATE MIKE - A MILLION TO ONE CHANCE!
AND A GREAT WAY TO END THE JOURNEY BACK HOME -
SINGING CANNED HEAT'S - 'ON THE ROAD AGAIN'......

MY 21ST BIRTHDAY

BACK HOME ON ENGLISH SOIL
I LEFT MY FEELINGS BACK IN DENMARK
ANNETTE - I STILL COULN'T FORGET HER

I BROKE UP, SADLY WITH MY GIRLFRIEND NINA
I HAD MOVED ON, MY LOVE FOR HER HAD GONE

A FEW MONTHS ON I MET UP WITH AN OLD GIRLFRIEND
WHO HAD JUST BROKEN OFF HER ENGAGEMENT
WE WENT OUT TOGETHER A PURELY PLATONIC ARRANGEMENT

THAT EVENTUALLY TURNED INTO AN INTENSE RELATIONSHIP
WITH FULL BLOWN BURNING PASSION AND DESIRE
AS JIM MORRISON OF 'THE DOORS' WOULD SING
"COME ON BABY LIGHT MY FIRE"

OUR FIRE WAS LIT! LYNN AND I WERE AN ITEM
WE HAD THAT EVERLASTING LOVING FEELING
I WAS ROCKING AND SHE WAS REELING

ON JUNE 8TH 1969 A BIG FAMILY PARTY
WAS ORGANIZED FOR MY 21ST BIRTHDAY
AT THE BROOKDALE INN, FAILSWORTH
BOTH MY EX-GIRLFRIEND NINA
& CURRENT GIRLFRIEND LYNN CAME
LIFE WOULD NEVER BE THE SAME AGAIN

LYNN HAD MOVED FROM HER MUM'S
INTO A SHARED FLAT
IN ABBOTSFORD ROAD, CHORLTON,
MANCHESTER WITH A WELSH GIRL
CALLED MORFRED & HER FIANCE ROY
(WHO SLEPT IN SEPARATE BEDROOMS)

THEY WERE TO BE MARRIED SOON
LYNN WAS LIKE THEIR CHAPERONE

I STAYED OVER THE NIGHT
THEY WENT BACK TO SOUTH WALES
TO PREPARE FOR THEIR WEDDING
& THE FROSTY FACED LANDLADY HAD
FOUND OUT

& TOLD US ON NO UNCERTAIN TERMS TO GET OUT
BUT MUCH WORSE SHE SAID THAT THE WELSH COUPLE
MORF & ROY HAD TO LEAVE TOO

WHAT WERE WE GOING TO DO?
LYNN'S MUM UNKNOWINGLY SAID TO ME
THAT SHE KNEW LYNN WOULD COME BACK HOME
& THAT SHE COULDN'T LIVE ON HER OWN

LYNN & I HITCH-HIKED ALL THE WAY
TO FISHGUARD, IN SOUTH WALES FOR THEIR WEDDING
& WHEN WE EVENTUALLY ARRIVED

THEY TOLD US THAT THE WEDDING HAD BEEN CALLED OFF
DUE TO SOME OLD FASHION RELIGEOUS REASON
ABOUT THEM LIVING TOGETHER - AS IF IT WAS TREASON

EVERYBODY LOOKED SO SAD
MORF & ROY HAD NEVER SLEPT TOGETHER
THEY WERE SAVING THEMSELVES FOR THEIR MARRIAGE

IT WAS THE SO CALLED PROMISCIOUS SIXTIES
& THE CHURCH WOULDN'T MARRY THEM!

LYNN & I JUST LAUGHED & LAUGHED AT THE IRONY OF IT ALL
IN THE ERA OF MAKE LOVE NOT WAR!
& WE DIDN'T HAVE THE HEART TO TELL THEM
THAT THEY HAD NO FLAT TO COME BACK TOO!

ACTUALLY WE WENT (TAIL BETWEEN OUR LEGS)
BACK TO THE FLAT TO BEG & PLEAD
WITH OL' FROSTY FACE WHAT HAD REALLY HAPPENED
SAYING THAT
IT WASN'T FAIR

& TO LET THE
INNOCENT
MORF & ROY
LIVE BACK THERE

& GUESS WHAT -
SHE RELUCTANTLY
AGREED......

WHEN WE WERE YOUNG (PART 1)

WE MADE LOVE

ON THE STEPS OF 'THE FREE TRADE HALL'
THE CONCERT AUDIENCE APPLAUDED US
AND CALLED FOR AN 'ENCORE'

WE MADE LOVE

BEHIND THE CHURCHYARD WALL
"GO FORTH!" GOD COMMANDED
AND GAVE AN ALMIGHTY RRROAR!!

WE MADE LOVE

IN THE DOORWAY OF A FAMOUS FLORISTS
WE WERE OBLIVIOUS TO THE PASSING MOTORISTS
THE RUSHING, PUSHING, HURRYING, SCURRYING
BUSINESS PEOPLE, SHOPPERS & TRAVEL TOURISTS

WE MADE LOVE

IN THE POURING RAIN
SPASHING IN THE PUDDLES —
JUST GOING INSANE

WE MADE LOVE

INBETWEEN THE GOALPOSTS
ON 'OLD TRAFFORD'S' HALLOWED FOOTBALL PITCH
AND JUDGING BY THE REACTION
FROM THE 'STRETFORD END'
WE GAVE THE BETTER DISPLAY —
& YOU CAN SEE THE RECORDED HIGHLIGHTS
ON SATURDAY NIGHT'S 'MATCH OF THE DAY'

WE MADE LOVE

IN THE TELEPHONE BOOTH
IGNORING THE EVER SO IMPATIENT QUEUE
(WHO HAD NOTHING BETTER TO DO)
WE HAD NO HANG UP'S - NOT US
WE WERE IN LOVE - IF ONLY THEY KNEW

WE MADE LOVE
AT EVERY HOUR OF THE NIGHT
AT EVER MINUTE OF THE DAY

IN FULL FLIGHT
IN FULL DISPLAY

WE WERE YOUNG
WE DIDN'T CARE
WE WOULD DO IT ANYWHERE......

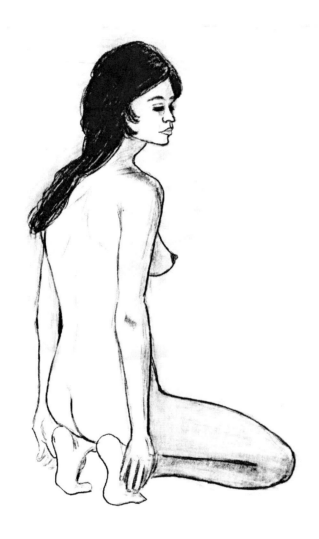

THE DARK SUBURBAN SKIES

HORNY HUMAN HANDS
TOUCHING NAKED HUMAN THIGHS

PINK BODIES
            AGAINST
                    THE DARK SUBURBAN SKIES

LEERING LOOKING EYES
SCANNING NAKED HUMAN FLESH

PINK BODIES
            AGAINST
                    THE DARK SUBURBAN SKIES

HUNGRY HUMAN MOUTHS
TASTING NAKED HUMAN BREASTS

PINK BODIES
            AGAINST
                    THE DARK SUBURBAN SKIES......

WHEN WE WERE YOUNG (PART 2)

WE MADE LOVE

IN THE CO-OP SUPERSTORE INBETWEEN THE SHOPPING TROLLEYS
AND THE CUT-PRICED CONSCIOUS HOUSEWIVES
(WHO DIDN'T KNOW THE PRICE OF LOVE)
WE ROLLED & TUMBLED ALL OVER THE FLOOR

WE MADE LOVE

ON THE BACKSEAT OF THE ALLNIGHT BUS
OVERSTATING OUR DESTINATION - TO THE TERMINUS!

WE MADE LOVE

IN THE LOCAL CINEMA TO 'THE SOUND OF MUSIC'
THE UNZIPPING OF ZIPS & THE CRACKLING OF OUR BUTTERKIST LIPS

WE MADE LOVE

ON THE WET GRASS - OVER THE LEA
BEHIND A DISCONCERTED COW & A SLIGHTLY EMBARRASSED TREE

WE MADE LOVE

EVER SO QUIETLY IN THE REFERENCE SECTION
OF THE LOCAL LIBRARY
AMIDST THE HUSHES, THE SHUSHES, THE HOT FLUSHES
AND THE LIBRARIAN'S OCCASIONAL BLUSHES

WE MADE LOVE

IN THE WINTER'S SNOW
FOUR ROSIE CHEEKS TINGLING ALL AGLOW

WE MADE LOVE

ANYWHERE & EVERWHERE
WE EXPLOITED EVERY POSITION IN COITION
WE CREATED & INNOVATED - WE EVEN ADDED
NEW CRAZES, NEW RAGES TO THE 'KARMA SUTRA'S' EROTIC PAGES
UNTIL THE DAY WE GOT WED
AND NOW WE ONLY MAKE LOVE
THE 'PROPER WAY' - IN BED!......

PREMONITION

ONE COLD WINTER'S NIGHT
MYSELF, MY HEAVILY PREGNANT GIRLFRIEND LYNN,
HER MUM IVY AND STEPFATHER CLIFF HAD GONE
TO A FAMILY WEDDING IN BOLLINGTON (MACCLESFIELD)

LATER THAT NIGHT AFTER SAYING OUR GOODBYES TO EVERYONE
WE WERE ABOUT TO LEAVE FOR HOME AROUND ABOUT MIDNIGHT
WHEN MY GIRLFRIEND SAID THAT SHE FELT VERY
NERVOUS AND LOOKED REALLY UPTIGHT

THEN PLEADED WITH ME SAYING THAT
SHE DIDN'T WANT TO GO BACK HOME IN HER STEPFATHER'S CAR
BECAUSE SHE FEARED THAT SOMETHING BAD WAS GOING TO HAPPEN

I EVENTUALLY PERSUADED HER TO COME
BECAUSE A TAXI FROM WHERE WE WERE
WOULD HAVE COST US A FORTUNE

ANYHOW AN HOUR OR SO ON
WE WERE NEAR HER MUM'S HOME (DROYLSDEN)
DRIVING INTO LUMB LANE, AUDENSHAW

WHEN SUDDENLY THROUGH THE ROLLING MIST,
A BIG BLACK CAR SUDDENLY SWERVED OUT OF CONTROL
THEN CAME SPEEDING TOWARDS US AND COLLIDED
INTO THE PASSENGER SIDE FRONT WING WHERE LYNN WAS SITTING

LYNN WAS SCREAMING HYSTERICALLY
AND KEPT SHOUTING OUT "I KNEW IT!, I KNEW IT!",
AND SHE HAD BROKEN ALL HER FINGER NAILS
HOLDING ONTO THE DASHBOARD

IT WAS A MIRACLE THAT NOBODY WAS HURT
ONLY SHOCKED AND BADLY SHAKEN
IT COULD HAVE BEEN FATAL

IF SHE HADN'T PREPARED HERSELF FOR THE IMPACT
HER 'PREMONITION' HAD STRANGLY COME TRUE
AND THE BABY WAS UNHARMED TOO!

LYNN AND I WERE MARRIED AT
ST. MARY'S CHURCH, DROYLSDEN 10 JAN 1970

WE HAD A BABY SON DAMIAN SCOTT
ON THE 23RD OF MAY THAT YEAR
WHO INCIDENTLY WAS ONE OF A TWIN
(THE OTHER WE LOST IN EARLY PREGNANCY)

MY WIFE LYNN WAS A TWIN TO HER BROTHER WAYNE
HER MUM WAS ALSO A TWIN TO HER SISTER LILLIAN
SO IF THE BABY WOULD HAVE SURVIVED
THERE WOULD HAVE BEEN
THREE GENERATIONS OF TWINS
BUT SADLY THIS WASN'T TO BE

WE HAD ANOTHER SON
NICHOLAS ALEXANDER
THREE YEARS LATER

WE GOT HIS NAME
AFTER WATCHING THE FILM
'NICHOLAS AND ALEXANDER'
ABOUT THE RUSSIAN REVOLUTION

AND THE BRUTAL & CRUEL
EXTERMINATION OF
THE TZAR NICHOLAS,
HIS WIFE AND CHILDREN BY THE
COMMUNIST REVOLUTIONARYS......

OUR GRANDAD

ONE NIGHT, OUR TELLY
WAS BEING CLOSELY OBSERVED
BY OUR EVER SUSPECTING GRANDAD

A JAZZ PIANIST OF GREAT RENOWN APPEARS
PLAYING FINE BLUES IN 'B' FLAT

"RRRUBBISH!!" SNORTS
OUR GRUMPY OL' GRANDAD

"WEV'E GORRA AN' OL' FELLA
AT THE VETERANS CLUB
CAN PLAY BETTER THAN THAT!"......

GRANDAD BREAK'S WIND

OUR GRANDAD WOULD SIT IN HIS CHAIR
BELCHIN', RIFTIN' AND BREAKIN' WIND

HE DIDN'T CARE
ANYMORE

HE WOULD JUST SIT THERE
IN HIS OL' ARMCHAIR

SUCKIN' MINTS
BELCHIN' RIFTIN' AND BREAKIN' WIND

PERHAPS IT WAS THE MINTS?
HE DIDN'T CARE
OUR GRANDAD

WHY SHOULD HE?
IT WAS HIS CHAIR......

THE DAY GRANDAD CAME TO VISIT

OUR NEW LOG-EFFECT GAS FIRE WAS DADS PRIDE AND JOY
"WONDERFULL PIECE OF ADVANCED TECHNOLOGY", HE'D GO ON
LIKE A KID WITH A BRAND NEW TOY

THEN ONE DAY OUR GRANDAD CAME TO VISIT
GRAND 'OL CHAP, WAR HERO, QUITE EXQUISITE

A MAN OF GREAT GRANDEUR, WISDOM AND WIT
ON THE BEST CHAIR BY THE FIRE HE'D ALWAYS SIT -
DOZIN', SNOOZIN', SNORIN' -
'COS THAT'S ALL GRANDAD WOULD DO ALL DAY

ANYHOW! ON THIS PARTICULAR HOT SUNNY SUMMER'S DAY,
ABOUT HALF PAST TWO, HALF WAY THRO' THE SUNDAY FILM,
RIGHT OUT OF THE BLUE, TO DAD'S DISMAY AND OURS TOO!

GRANDAD SUDDENLY, WITHOUT WARNING - SHOT UP
AND FORGETTING HIMSELF - AS HE ALWAYS DID
CLEARED HIS THROAT "A HUMM! - A CCARRRRRRAGHHH!!"
TOOK AIM AND - "OH! NO!" SHOUTED DAD, "NO! GRANDAD NNO!!!"
SPIT! - TOO LATE FOR OUR ACE MARKSMAN A DIRECT HIT!

"CAN'T FOOL 'OL GRANDAD", HE'D SAY
WITHOUT REALISING HIS FOLLY -
"DAM GAS FIRES, CAN'T BEAT THE 'OL COAL UN'S - REAL UN'S"
HE'D GO ON GRUMBLIN' IN HIS GRANDAD SORT OF WAY
THEN SLUMP BACK IN HIS CHAIR - BOTH BLAMELESS AND SHAMELESS
TO DOZE THE SLEEPY AFTERNOON AWAY....

GRANDAD (OUR HERO)

EVERY OTHER SUNDAY, OUR GRANDAD WOULD COME FOR TEA
HE NEVER FAILED TO ENTERTAIN MY BROTHERS AND ME
HE USED TO SINGALONG WITH THE 'ADAMS SINGERS' ON THE RADIO
SONGS LIKE "SOUNDS OF THE SEA, BOBBIN' UP AND DOWN LIKE ME"

AND "I WOULDN'T LEAVE MY LITTLE WOODEN HUT, FOR YOU SUGAR"
HE WAS A RIGHT OL' RUM BUGGER!

ONE DAY OUR DAD BOUGHT A SECOND HAND 'GRUNDIG TAPE RECORDER'
OFF 'GREY MARE LANE MARKET' - HE HAD US ALL SINGIN' & LARKIN'
GRANDAD WOULD SING "BY THE LIGHT OF THE SILVERY MOON"
& US KIDS WOULD BACK HIM & SING -
"SILVEREE MOON, SILVEREE MOON"
IT WAS HILARIOUS, ALTHOUGH GRANDAD WAS DEADLY SERIOUS

I REMEMBER DAD ONCE REWINDING & PLAYING BACK THE TAPE
WITH FRANK SINATRA SINGING 'MY WAY'
OUR GRANDAD WAS CONVINCED THAT IT WAS HIM SINGING 'HIS WAY'

PLAYING DARTS WAS ANOTHER PASSION OF HIS
WE WOULD PLAY ROUND THE BOARD
AND JUST WHEN YOU WERE GOING TO THROW THAT WINNING DART
GRANDAD WOULD, AS USUAL, COUGH, BELCH AND FART!
THUS BLOWIN' YOU WELL OFF COURSE - WE'D ALL CURSE!

ESPECIALLY WHEN HE THREW THAT WINNING ARROW
INTO THE BULLSEYE
GIVING A WICKED GRIN & SAYING -
"NOT BAD FER AN OL' MAN WITH ONE EYE!"
HE WAS EVEN WORSE AT CARDS -
TWISTIN' OL' BUGGER - A REAL CHARACTER

PRIVATE A. PRESTBURY No.29101 OF THE 'ROYAL WELSH FUSILIERS'
ENTRENCHED IN THE INTENSE BATTLE ACTION OF WORLD WAR ONE
GOT WOUNDED IN HIS ARM IN THE INFAMOUS BATTLE OF THE 'SOMME'

ALTHOUGH HE NEVER EVER TALKED ABOUT THE SO CALLED GREAT WAR
TOO PAINFUL WAS THE TRAUMA, TOO BITTER WAS THE MEMORY
(HE APPARENTLY LOST MOST OF HIS MATES IN ONE TRAGIC DAY)

HE WAS OUR HERO -
NOTHING EVER WORRIED HIM OR GOT HIM DOWN AFTER THE WAR
ALTHOUGH SMALL IN STATURE TO US KIDS HE WAS A BIG MAN
THEY SAY THAT OLD SOLDIERS NEVER DIE, THEY JUST FADE AWAY
AND FADE AWAY HE DID AT 83 YEARS OF AGE......

ROYAL WELSH FUSILIERS 1914
(GRANDAD FIRST LEFT 2ND ROW AT THE BACK)

YOU, OLD MAN
(WITH GREY WHISKERS & CLOTH CAP)

YOU, OLD MAN WITH GREY WHISKERS & CLOTH CAP
SPEAK OF THE PAST
REMINISCENT OF THE DAYS
THAT HAVE GONE BY SO FAST

NOW YOU'RE SUSPENDED & CAN'T GO BACK
THE FUTURE HOLDS NO INTEREST
ALL YOU WANT IS THE PAST

THOSE YEARS OF WAR-TIME EXPERIENCE
BLOODSHED, TRAGEDY & DESTRUCTION

TIMES OF RECESSION,
OPPRESSION & THE DEPRESSION
HARDSHIP, POVERTY, DESTITUTION,
DESPAIR, DEPRIVATION & DESOLATION

SENTIMENTAL TEARS OF HAPPINESS
ROLL DOWN YOUR WRINKLED FACE
REFLECTING PAST LOVE AFFAIRS,
ROMANCES, OLD FLAMES, OLD WAYS

CELEBRATING, REJOICING, MERRYMAKING
THE LAUGHING, SINGING,
DRINKING, DANCING DAYS

DAYS OF HOPE, HOURS OF GLORY
& YOU HAVE LIVED TO TELL THE STORY
YOU, OLD MAN KEPT ON GOING
YOUR WILL TO LIVE WAS GLOWING
YOUR HEART & SOUL WERE GROWING

STRONGER, HEALING, MENDING
UNYIELDING, DEFENDING, NEVERENDING

& NOW YOU, OLD MAN WITH GREY WHISKERS & CLOTH CAP
ARE TIRED, WEARY, LISTLESS & SAD
YOU REALISE THOSE YESTERYEARS WEREN'T ALL BAD

SUSPENDED FOREVER & CAN'T GO BACK
THE FUTURE HOLDS NO INTEREST

ALL YOU WANT BACK IS THE PAST.....

THE FORGOTTEN YEARS

I AM THE TRAIN
    THE MEMORABILIA EXPRESS
        MOVING THROUGH
            THE YESTERYEARS
                OF MY LIFE

PASSING
    THROUGH
        THE DISTANT
            TUNNELS OF LOVE

EACH ONE BEARING
    EACH ONE CARING
        EACH ONE TEARING
            EACH ONE WEARING
                THE YEARS OF MY LIFE

LOOKING BACK
    DOWN THE TRACK
        PASSING ROMANCES
            PASSING PHASES

GOING
    THROUGH
        THE MAZES
            OF MY MIND

STOPPING
    AT STATIONS
        EXCHANGING RELATIONS
            SEEKING NEW EXPERIENCES
          AND SENSATIONS

ANOTHER DAY GONE
    ANOTHER DAY OLDER
        A LITTLE MORE WISE
            A LITTLE BIT BOLDER

MEMORIES
    JUST MEMORIES
        IS ALL YOU HAVE
            PAST UPON PAST
              GOING FAST
                GOING FAST

```
BUT
    NO RETURNING
        NO REGRESSING
            MUST KEEP GOING
                KEEP PROGRESSING

CREATING
    INNOVATING
        MOTIVATING
            FORWARDS
                ONWARDS
                    TOWARDS
                        MY DESTINATION

AND
    UNTIL MY DESTINATION
        THE FORGOTTEN YEARS
            OF MY LIFE
                HAVE YET
                    TO BE FORGOTTEN......
```

BEATLES & STONES ETC.

ALONG WITH BOB DYLAN AND ELVIS PRESLEY
THE BEATLES AND THE ROLLING STONES DOMINATED THE SIXTIES

THE BEATLES –
WERE ALWAYS ONE STEP AHEAD OF THE FIELD
SO CREATIVE AND INVENTIVE - GREAT LYRICS - A SENSATION
FROM 'YESTERDAY' TO 'TOMORROW NEVER KNOWS'
ONTO 'A DAY IN A LIFE' TO 'LUCY IN THE SKY WITH DIAMONDS'
'HEY JUDE' AND 'LADY MADONNA', 'GET BACK' AND 'LET IT BE'
ALL SIXTIES ROCK CLASSICS

THE ROLLING STONES –
WERE MUCH MORE RAUNCHY AND REBELLIOUS
BOTH EXCITING AND TERRIFIC TO WATCH - A REVELATION
'I CAN'T GET NO SATISFACTION' TO 'PAINT IT BLACK'
'RUBY TUESDAY' AND 'JUMPING JACK FLASH'
'HONKY TONK WOMAN' AND 'GIMME SHELTER'
THEIR OUTPUT YOU COULDN'T FAULTER

BOB DYLAN –
WAS SHEER POETRY WITH HIS ZANY,
MINDBLOWING AND MINDBENDING LYRICS - A CULTURAL REVOLUTION
FROM 'BLOWIN' IN THE WIND' TO 'A HARD RAIN'S A-GONNA-FALL'
'LIKE A ROLLIN' STONE' AND 'IT'S ALL OVER NOW, BABY BLUE'
'JOHN WESLEY HARDING', 'LAY LADY LAY' SHOWN US THE WAY

ELVIS PRESLEY –
WAS THE KING OF ROCK & ROLL
WITH HIS COSMIC AURA AND MISSISSIPPI DRAWL
FROM 'JAILHOUSE ROCK' TO 'KING CREOLE'
'GIRL OF MY BEST FRIEND' TO 'IT'S NOW OR NEVER',
'IN THE GHETTO', 'AMERICAN TRILOGY', AND 'SUSPICIOUS MINDS'
HE WAS A ROCK GOD FROM ANOTHER PLANET - A GIANT OF THE TIMES

THESE ICONS, ROCK LEGENDS, ENHANCED THE QUALITY OF OUR LIVES
AND MADE OUR WORLD A MUCH PLEASUREABLE PLACE TO ENDEAR......

'THE KING' ELVIS PRESLEY

DAVID PRESTBURY

WAS BORN IN GREAT ANCOATS, MANCHESTER, ENGLAND
SPENT FIRST TWO YEARS OF HIS LIFE IN GORTON, MANCHESTER 18
HIS BOYHOOD YEARS IN CLAYTON, (UNTIL 15) MANCHESTER 11
& THE REST OF HIS TEENAGE YEARS IN FAILSWORTH, MANCHESTER

HAS LIVED IN BOWKER VALE, WHITEFIELD & PRESTWICH
FOR TWENTY YEARS OR SO (ALL NORTH MANCHESTER AREAS)
AND IS NOW LIVING BACK IN FAILSWORTH, MANCHESTER

WAS (UN) EDUCATED AT 'RAVENSBURY STREET',
SEC. SCHOOL IN CLAYTON, MANCHESTER 11
LEFT SCHOOL AT 15 TO BECOME AN APPRENTICE COMPOSITOR
THEN ON TO BE A JOURNEYMAN COMPOSITOR (PRINTER)

WENT TO COLLEGE OF ART & DESIGN, MANCHESTER STUDIED
PHOTOGRAPHIC PRINTING
TECHNIQUES -
TO BE A FULLY QUALIFIED
FILM MAKE UP ARTIST

APART FROM BEING A PRINTER -
DAVE HAS HAD A VARIETY OF
JOBS:
POSTMAN, PROGRESS CHASER,
PRODUCTION CONTROLLER,
ENGINEERING
STOREKEEPER/BUYER
AND HAS CURRENTLY TAKEN
EARLY RETIREMENT
TO BECOME A CARER & FULL
TIME WRITER

DAVE HAS HAD POEMS PUBLISHED IN VARIOUS MAGAZINES:
WRITE ON, ALLUSIONS, FLY BY NIGHT ETC.
BEEN INVOLVED IN A ROADSHOW 'THE LAST WORD'
FROM THE COMMONWORD WRITER'S WORKSHOP, MANCHESTER.
DOING READINGS & SKETCHES AT VARIOUS VENUES,
INCLUDING FOLK CLUBS, LIBRAYS, CULTURAL & COMMUNITY CENTRES
IN THE GREATER MANCHESTER & LANCASHIRE AREAS

ALSO DONE READINGS -
AT NOTTINGHAM UNIVERSITY'S WRITER'S FESTIVAL
REPRESENTING COMMONWORD WRITER'S WORKSHOP,

MANCHESTER - FOR WRITER'S CLUBS THROUGHOUT THE COUNTRY
AND BELLE VUE PEOPLES FESTIVAL, MANCHESTER.
BEEN A MEMBER OF 'THE VALLEY POETS'
WITH FELLOW POET & LIFE LONG FRIEND 'ALAN BUTTERWORTH'
(THAT EVOLVED FROM 'THE ORGAN INN', HOLLINGWORTH, HYDE)

DAVE HAS ALSO BEEN INVOLVED IN A VARIETY SHOW
- AS A DOUBLE ACT WITH FELLOW WRITER ALAN BUTTERWORTH
(FROM THE VALLEY POETS) CALLED 'PAVEMENT ARTISTES'
AT THE GUIDE BRIDGE THEATRE, ASHTON-U-LYNE, GTR. MANCHESTER

APART FROM WRITING POETRY DAVE'S OTHER INTERESTS
INCLUDE ART (DRAWING & PAINTING), PHOTOGRAPHY
& NIGHT CLUBBING WITH HIS MATES AROUND
MANCHESTER & BURY AREAS

- THIS IS DAVE'S FOLLOW UP BOOK TO THE SUCCESSFULL
'*THE DONKEY STONE & DOLLY BLUE DAYS*'
SET IN & AROUND MANCHESTER IN THE LATE 1950'S
FIRST EDITION PUBLISHED 1998 BY -
THE 'CASTLE OF DREAMS' PUBLISHING CO., DARLINGTON.
SPECIAL EDITION PUBLISHED BY DAVID PRESTBURY 2008

HE IS CURRENTLY WORKING ON HIS NEXT BOOK OF POETRY -
'*HIDDEN BY THE CLOUDS*' DEEP STUFF BY D. PRESTBURY......

DAVE IN CHILL OUT MOOD - 2007

Printed in the United Kingdom
by Lightning Source UK Ltd.
134742UK00001B/57-62/P